Aha!

More Out of the Box Revelations

By

Jeannie Boatright

Copyright © 2016 Jeannie Boatright

All rights reserved.

Published by Truth Rejoices

truthrejoices.com

ISBN-10: 09974668-1-2
ISBN-13: 978-0-9974668-1-2

Dedications

I originally had a short dedication page, but since I started writing this book many experiences and divine appointments have altered both my plans and my dedications.

First and foremost, I dedicate this book to my wonderful Savior and best friend Jesus Christ. You are my first love and the author and finisher of my faith. May you be glorified!

I dedicate this book to my children Joshua, Shanna, Rebekah, and Caleb. You are my greatest treasures in this life, and I am so very proud of each of you! You are all amazing overcomers with incredible destinies! May you each continue to prosper in all God has for you!

To Frances Boatright: Mom, you were a prayer warrior and loved the Lord to the end. You taught me to turn to the Lord in all circumstances and to consider others better than myself. You saw every obstacle as an opportunity and had a heart for evangelism that impacted all with whom you came in contact. I am so thankful for your Christian influence. I look forward to the day when I will see you again in Heaven's glory.

To my father Mody Boatright: Dad, we have both grown so much, especially during these past few years as I have helped you take care of Mom and Judy, my special needs sister. At first, I couldn't understand why you wouldn't put Mom in a care center when her health deteriorated to the point that she wasn't in her right mind, and we had to change and often feed her. But now I understand. Thank you for giving me a glimpse of how Christ loves us (His bride) in how you loved Mom. As you told me, "Your mother wants to be home. And I want her home, so we will do whatever we have to do to make that happen!" You were beside Mom from the day you wed to the night she left this earth. Thank you for modeling love, perseverance, and commitment.

To my baby brother Mark: When Mom went into the hospice unit a week before she died, I had no idea you were going to spend the last night of your life across the hall from her. We had held onto hopes of your recovery until earlier that morning. Years ago, God prepared a permanent place for you when Mom brought you home from Mrs. Barker's foster care. In 2014, you were privileged to welcome Mom home to Heaven one day after your arrival. You were an example of perseverance and optimism for all of us. I always admired your father's heart. You loved your son and daughter dearly, and everyone who knew you was touched by your love and commitment to them. You might have gone to Heaven first, but all of us will one day join you. I know you are having a blast!

To my amazing daughter Rebekah and my wonderful friends Jan Luke, Lakendra Lewis, Terry Rendon, and

Marie Hubbard, who have each contributed your time and talents toward the editing of this book.

To my pastors Mark and Tamara Patterson and my River of Life church family: Thank you for your love, encouragement, and support during a very difficult season. You are all amazing! I am so thankful that God brought all of you into my life!

Table of Contents

1. Finding Me-*God's Loving Pursuit*   *1*

2. What Is Your Plumb Line-*Christian Growth*   *7*

3. It Is Finished!-*Healing*   *16*

4. Let Me Be God-*Trusting God*   *24*

5. Unseen Ears-*Blessing*   *31*

6. S.O.S.-*Relying on God*   *41*

7. Super-*Overcoming*   *49*

8. Stretch Marks-*Growth*   *56*

9. The Doll-*God's Timing*   *63*

10. Something Special for Everyone-*Supply*   *71*

11. Friendly Captivity-*Freedom*   *79*

12. Come Forth-*Deliverance*   *87*

13. The Hummingbird-*Helping Others*   *94*

14. Perfect Peace-*Direction*   *100*

15. Humane-*Enabling*   *109*

16. Breaking the Power-*Overcoming Temptation*   *117*

17. Disappointment-*Comfort*   126

18. Releasing the Debt-*Forgiveness*   132

19. Revisiting the Broken Places-*Restoration*   140

20. What Is It?-*Direction*   149

21. The Red Sea-*Trust*   155

22. The Flow-*Provision*   163

23. 911-*Prayer*   170

24. From Fear to Faith-*Moving in Faith*   176

25. Too Fast Too Soon-*Giving*   182

26. I'll Get There First-*Facing Death*   188

27. A Lesson From a Gecko-*Spiritual Desire*   195

28. Time to Fly   201

Preface

In my last book, *Temper Tantrums With God and Other Out of the Box Revelations,* I shared many experiences about when God gave me life-giving revelations when I was arguing with Him in the midst of difficult situations. This book has similar Aha moments, but much less drama. Thankfully, God doesn't just speak in the storms. He speaks to our hearts all the time.

Although I gave my life to Christ when I was young, for almost thirty years I suffered from spiritual dyslexia. I honestly thought *I* was in control. I viewed God as a judgmental, angry, taskmaster whom I could never please so I served Him out of fear instead of love. Since I didn't trust Him or His heart for me, I would vacillate between trying to earn His love and approval to outright challenging Him to try to make Him do things my way.

Thankfully, my merciful, sweet Lord never gave up on me. He just continued to love me and speak life to me as He met me in amazing ways and revealed His character and my identity. As I learned more about His love, my value, and my purpose, I was able to leave the box of guilt, shame, self-protection, self-righteousness, unworthiness, control, pride, false identity, manipulation, and fear in which I had been confined and experience more freedom than I ever thought possible.

As you read more of my "Out of the Box" God encounters, I pray that your heart and mind would be opened to receive more understanding of His unconditional love and His care and commitment to you. May you be abundantly blessed as you take hold of all God has for you as you experience your personal Aha moments with Him.

Hearing God's Voice

In my last book I mentioned that I first had knowingly heard God's voice when I had a divine encounter in a hospital room. But, later on, I realized that I had been hearing Him speak to my heart from childhood. The main reason I didn't know it was Him was because I was raised in a church that believed that God quit speaking to man after the last disciple died. Thankfully, I now know that He not only speaks, but He does it through a variety of ways.

Sometimes God speaks to me through a gut feeling that lets me know that something is not quite right. At other times it's just in knowing I need to do a certain thing or go to a certain place. Sometimes His voice is in actual words I hear in my mind, giving me encouragement, confirmation, or instruction. On a few occasions, it sounded like a letter that was being read in my head. Often, it's through a picture or vision with understanding or through a dream with an interpretation. On many occasions, His words that have brought me hope or clarity in direction have been spoken to me through a friend or even a stranger.

No matter how He chooses to speak, God speaks words of love, life, truth, hope, encouragement, instruction, and direction. In each case it is always in total agreement with the Bible.

Instead of rushing or pushing us, His voice brings peace and quiets us, reminding us to always trust instead of worrying. Instead of inciting fear, He will firmly direct us and calm us with words of His perfect love. His words will encourage us and validate our true identity. They will restore our wounded souls by bringing clarity in the midst of confusion and comfort in the midst of heartache, distress, or chaos.

Although He will warn and convict us, God does not condemn us because He is always for us and not against us. He has a huge heart for us and is continually leading us and cheering us on to fulfill the plans that He has destined for us. "For I know the thoughts that I think toward you, says the LORD, thoughts of peace and not of evil, to give you a future and a hope" Jeremiah 29:11

Finding Me

The day I went to see the newest Disney flick with my kids I had no idea I was walking into a divine appointment. But I have since learned that the Lord can and will use absolutely anything to reach us: people, places, events, books—even an animated fish story.

As a single mother, I went through a season marked by so much disappointment, I was feeling abandoned. Eventually I became so depressed I didn't want to leave the house. I might have stayed that way had I not promised to take my children to see *Finding Nemo*. Thankfully, my merciful Father had other plans.

The movie began with a clown fish couple admiring their new home and clutch of eggs in the Great Barrier Reef. However, bliss soon turns to horror when a barracuda attacks their home. When Marlin, the father, regains consciousness, his hopes and dreams of moments before are shattered as he realizes his wife is dead and the eggs are gone—that is—all but one. Marlin then rushes to the one remaining egg. As he cradles it in his fins, he tenderly speaks from the depth of his paternal heart: "There, there, there. It's okay. Daddy's here. Daddy's got you. I promise I won't ever let anything happen to you." As Marlin spoke those loving words to the still unhatched Nemo, my Heavenly Father repeated them in my heart: *"It's okay. Daddy's here. Daddy's got you. I won't let anything happen to you!"* My Heavenly Father's tender, loving words poured hope and assurance into my wounded spirit; they opened my soul to receive His heart for me throughout the rest of the movie.

Although God is not fear-driven or overprotective, as Marlin became, He similarly is motivated by love. The depth of Marlin's love for his son becomes apparent when Nemo's life radically changes after a single act of defiance gets him captured and placed in a fish tank in Sydney, Australia. As I witnessed Marlin risking everything and braving numerous hazards in his relentless pursuit of his "beloved boy," I was flooded with a greater understanding of how God pursues us in order to bring us a two-fold freedom. God not only frees us *from* our sin and bondages, He also frees us *for* a relationship with Him.

As I heard the passion in Marlin's voice when calling his son's name, I relived some of the chapters of my own life. Although I had been aware of God's existence since childhood, I had never thought about His loving persistence in pursuing me. As I sat in the theatre that afternoon revisiting my past, I could clearly see the

Lord's loving faithfulness as He fought off vicious attackers, pulled me out of precarious situations, and drew me closer to His heart.

I continued to sit through the film in wide-eyed wonder as I marveled at all the Lord had brought me through. He had risked so much for me, especially through the sacrifice of His own son on Calvary, in order to bring me salvation and ultimate freedom. As new revelations of His unconditional love washed over me, it was no little fish story that I was seeing that day. For what was playing on the screen before my eyes in the theatre wasn't nearly as dramatic as the story unfolding in my heart. For me, Marlin wasn't just *finding Nemo*. My Daddy God was *finding me*!

♥ *Heart Encounter* ♥

1. God is in relentless pursuit of us and for us, so much so that He was willing to sacrifice in the greatest way possible; which is what He did when He gave us Jesus. The Bible tells us "For God so greatly loved and dearly prized the world that He [even] gave up His only begotten (unique) Son, so that whoever believes in (trusts in, clings to, relies on) Him shall not perish (come to destruction, be lost) but have eternal (everlasting) life" John 3:16 (AMP). For many years, I thought I had to continuously earn my

salvation. Learning that Jesus' sacrifice on the cross paid for all of my sins (past, present, and future) released me to serve Him out of love instead of guilt, fear, and obligation. It is so wonderful to know that because of Jesus, the price for our sins, has already been paid, once and for all, and our freedom has been won! All we have to do is receive God's free gift of grace. Have you received God's precious gift?

2. When we receive Christ as our Savior, although we are set free from the penalty of sin (death, hell, and the grave), we can still be held captive in many areas of our lives. Yet, even then, the relentless love of the Father continues to draw us closer in order to bring us freedom and truth. Marlin's intent in rescuing Nemo was not to prove himself or to teach his son a lesson. He desired Nemo to be free just because he loved him. Do you believe God wants you to be free just because He loves you? Explain.

3. For many years, it was difficult for me to trust God's intentions, because I struggled with believing He loved me. But Romans 5:8 clearly reveals His heart: "But God shows *and* clearly proves His [own] love for us by the fact that while we were still sinners, Christ (the Messiah, the Anointed One) died for us" (AMP). God's drawing of our hearts begins before we

even know Him. He woos us to salvation and establishes a relationship with us, but that is only the beginning. Because of His undying passion for us, He continues to pursue our hearts, bringing us to greater places of freedom and deeper intimacy (into-me-you-see) with Him for the rest of our lives. Now I call that *true* love, don't you?

Just as Marlin pursued Nemo, our Heavenly Father is in constant pursuit of us. He flashes neon lights in the sky with every sunset sending forth a message of His presence as He tucks us in for another night under a blanket of stars. But the One who never slumbers nor sleeps not only meets us where we are, He also meets us where we *will be*. For He is constantly moving through time and space orchestrating divine appointments in order to free us from captivity and move closer to our hearts. "Behold what manner of love the Father has bestowed on us, that we should be called children of God!" (1John 3:1).

Let's Pray:

Father God, thank you for your unfathomable love for me. I am awed that you not only desire my freedom, but that you desire my companionship as well. Thank you for giving the ultimate sacrifice of your Son. I receive your free gift and welcome Jesus Christ into my heart as my Lord and Savior. I am also so very grateful that you are determined to meet me every day in every way in order to bring freedom and victory to all aspects of my life, for the rest of my life. I look forward to developing a deeper relationship and more intimacy with you as we walk through this life together. In Jesus' Name…Amen!

Reflections:

_____

_____

_____

_____

_____

_____

_____

_____

What Is Your Plumb Line?

I learned a lesson about Christian growth when my husband Joe and I bought our first house; not so much in the purchase of the home as in the repairs that transpired shortly afterwards.

Isn't it amazing how before you sign the deed, a place can look so perfect, then you realize there are numerous problems once the rose-colored glasses and the furniture are removed? In our case there was such a contrast, we were not only shocked but also overwhelmed. Walls that seemed to gleam before were now dingy. Doors were warped and cabinets and counter tops had obvious water damage. I continued to walk through the house, shaking my head in disbelief, thinking to myself, "How on earth could I have missed this stuff!?" But after rounding the corner of the master bath I came to a complete stop. As my eyes fixed on a 6X6 inch hole in the drywall, I couldn't help but wonder if my next pet would be a seeing-eye dog.

Since revelation can often bring about renovation, it was time get busy. So with the help of my husband Joe's parents we set to work scrubbing and painting. The living room and bedrooms soon took on a fresh clean look, but the other home improvements would have to wait until a later date. (Thankfully for some of the repairs, later, only meant days when my best friend Lori called and offered her assistance.) I'm not sure if the reason we accepted Lori's offer was due to our lack of inexperience or her home improvement skills and experience. But after glancing at the crooked book shelf Joe had recently built, and recalling the $100 we'd just paid for the ER stitches he acquired when he sliced his hand open while calking the bathroom, we readily accepted her offer.

As soon as Lori arrived, it was unanimously decided that we would tackle the master bathroom first—besides being small, it was tucked away in the back of the house, making it a great place to experiment. When I suggested that we cover the wall with material; Lori responded with a "You've gotta be kidding" look. It was obvious that her creative juices were flowing because she began to salivate as she informed me that it was time to learn the fine art of screening and spackling. Since I'm the kind of gal who can take a hint (or in this case, an all-out command), the next morning Lori and I hit the hardware aisle at the local department store before setting to work on the bathroom. We patched the hole in the wall with little difficulty, and then swirled the lower third of it with a thick pattern to cover up the obvious discrepancy in texture. We then bought base boards, chair railing, and wallpaper to give the room a "touch of elegance," which had apparently taken on a new level of importance since the wall was so close to the toilet it could end up with knee imprints.

As Lori and I labored, I acquired an assortment of new skills. Besides patching holes, which would become invaluable knowledge in the future (gotta love those kids), I learned how to cut baseboards, use a hammer "correctly," and apply wood filler. I also expanded my vocabulary to include terminology such as miter box, miter saw, nail punch, and liquid nails. However, the most valuable information I acquired during our home improvement project concerned the function of the plumb line.

For those of you who are unfamiliar with the term, a plumb line is a tool composed of a weighted plastic housing containing string and red chalk that is used for hanging wallpaper. Similar to a measuring tape, the chalk coated string is pulled out of its casing and the tip is placed on the top of the wall as the weighted housing is carefully dropped. When the user pinches, pulls back, and then releases the middle of the string, a straight line is left on the wall. Since walls and ceilings are rarely even, the plumb line is of vital importance, for if the mark on the wall isn't straight, not only will the first piece of wallpaper be crooked; every subsequent piece will be off kilter as well.

As I used this invaluable tool, the Lord began to speak to my heart about how the plumb line relates to the Bible concerning the restoration of our lives. As God begins to bring revelation, we become aware that the world, our thinking, and the patterns in our lives are off kilter. It is vitally important for you and I to have the reference point of the Word of God to align us with the truth so we can be centered in God's will concerning our actions, decisions, and relationships. I also think it's interesting that the chalk in my plumb line is red because it reminds me that I need to keep trusting in the shed blood of Christ to change me, rather than trusting in my own abilities.

Through the miracle of the cross God has given us beautiful new houses. Although our deeds have been paid in full, once the Holy Spirit opens our spiritual eyes it's easy to get overwhelmed with the *home improvements*, especially if we think we are solely responsible for the repairs. It is important that we keep in mind that although some things will be quick fixes, others will require more time, grace, and wisdom—all of which God has in endless supply. In the restoration process, we can confidently rest in the assurance of God's love and faithfulness. Not only has He committed to never leave nor forsake us, He has also given us the Holy Spirit, Christian fellowship, and the Bible (our plumb line) to enable us to do everything He has for us to do. If we continue to place our trust and hope in Him—in time— even the least visible and most damaged places in our "houses" will radiate with new elegance.

♥ *Heart Encounter* ♥

1. Think back to when you first accepted Christ as your Savior. What are some words you would use to describe your experience?

2. I can still remember the night I accepted Christ as if it were yesterday. Not only was I so full of joy I couldn't quit smiling, I felt so clean and pure I honestly thought I would never sin again. Imagine how disappointed I was the next day when I told a lie and was hit with the reality that being presented with a new life and purified through the righteousness of Christ did not erase all of my old flaws. At what point did you realize that your spiritual house, though new, still needed repairs?

3. In Philippians 1:6, Paul states "And I am convinced *and* sure of this very thing, that He Who began a good work in you will continue until the day of Jesus Christ

[right up to the time of His return], developing [that good work] *and* perfecting *and* bringing it to full completion in you" (AMP). It was many years before I learned that there was a difference between salvation and sanctification. Through salvation you and I inherit the righteousness of Christ, but through sanctification we grow in the character of Christ. What are some areas in your life where you notice the sanctification process at work?

4. I mentioned earlier the importance of the plumb line when Lori and I were transforming the bathroom, and I related how the plumb line can symbolize the Word of God. Unfortunately, I used to be a mess and live in a mess because I was ignorant about what the Bible says. If you and I don't know what God's Word says, what will be our measuring line?

5. Unfortunately, many of us measure ourselves and make our decisions by the counsel of the world or generational beliefs that have passed through our families. I actually had a Christian friend in high school whose grandmother told her she had to sleep with her father because she was his property. Now, exactly where does that fit into God's Word?! Although that might be an extreme example, I can think of many lies I used to believe about God,

relationships, and myself because I didn't know what the Word says. Can you identify false teachings which deceived you because you didn't know truth from the Bible? If so, what are some of them?

6. Proverb 24:3-4 instructs "Through skillful *and* godly Wisdom is a house (a life, a home, a family) built, and by understanding it is established [on a sound and good foundation], And by knowledge shall its chambers [of every area] be filled with all precious and pleasant riches" (AMP). When I didn't know how to make the repairs, the Lord sent me help. God sends us continuous help in the person of the Holy Spirit. He also will bring other believers into our lives to encourage us and counsel us and help us grow. But in order to receive counsel we must choose to hear with our hearts as well as our heads and stay teachable. Have you opened your heart to receive the counsel of the Holy Spirit, as well as the encouragement and sometimes admonition of others?

7. The other day, the Holy Spirit revealed to me an unhealthy relational pattern in my life. I immediately began to beat myself up. The Lord then tenderly spoke to my Spirit, "It's not about condemnation; it's about completion." All condemnation left and I was free to listen to and receive truth and wisdom

concerning my situation. Is the Holy Spirit highlighting a lie or pattern that has been hindering your growth? If so, what is He showing you?

Every day I become more aware of necessary changes I need to make to be formed into the image of my Savior. Although I am secure in knowing that God loves me just as I am, I am also aware that He loves me too much to let me stay the way I am now. In Matthew 5:16 we are told to "Let your light so shine before men that they may see your moral excellence *and* your praiseworthy, noble, *and* good deeds and recognize *and* honor *and* praise *and* glorify your Father who is in heaven"(AMP).

As God's children, you and I are not to have a house that is merely livable, but a house that reflects light—the light of His Son. May our lights shine bright as we stay in the Word (our plumb line), remain teachable, and above all else, trust that the Lord is faithful to complete the work He has begun in us.

Let's Pray:

Precious Lord, thank you for blessing me with this house. I realize that although I have been made new by the cleansing blood of Jesus, there are "home improvements" that are necessary for my continued growth. Illuminate Your Word, and bring me wisdom through Your Holy Spirit and wise counsel from others. Thank you for desiring what is best for me. I give you permission to remodel every room in "my house" to reflect *Your* glory. Help me to be available and patient in the process. In Jesus' Name...Amen!

Reflections:

_____

_____

_____

_____

_____

_____

_____

_____

_____

It Is Finished

I remember staring out of the window of my first grade classroom as Mom was loaded into an ambulance. I bolted out of the door and headed toward home, but my teacher ran after me and apprehended me. I felt so helpless.

Mom was sick so often. Her doctor didn't expect her to live past her thirties. Later that night, Dad snuck me into her hospital room. When he heard the doctor approaching the door, Dad had me hide under the bed. The doctor immediately discovered me But instead of scolding me, he showed compassion and let me stay a while longer. Later on that night, as I was curled up back home in my bed, I once again, wondered if I had just seen my mother for the very last time.

But God had other plans and Mom's health improved. Except for reoccurring headaches, frequent naps, and some weakness, she seemed to function pretty well for a quite few years. However, in her forties her health again rapidly declined. The first diagnosis was multiple sclerosis. Then added to that, was a severe immune system disorder, most likely resulting from what the doctors believed to be pesticide poisoning.

After a disheartening stay at Mayo Clinic and a longer stay in the hospital at the Environmental Health Center in Dallas, Texas, Mom was sent home to live out the rest of her days. She survived by taking shots for everything she ate or was exposed to, eating organic food that was flown in from Dallas and Houston, and using oxygen when needed. Since she was so highly allergic to absolutely everything, she had to live in a contained environment in the back bedroom of the house with her air purifier. Even the simplest routine was exhausting to her.

Mom slowly began to get better. However, because of her severe central nervous system reactions, even during her short outings she had to take her shots with her and carry a small metal chair to sit on since she was allergic to the phenol in plastic and the formaldehyde in stuffed furniture.

Even though she endured much suffering, I don't ever remember Mom complaining, which was quite opposite of how I reacted when I later went through similar medical conditions. It would be six years before Mom was healed. Thankfully, it was only four for me.

As I mentioned in my first book, in 1986, after being anointed with oil and receiving prayer, I was miraculously healed, threw away a $1,000 worth of medication, and walked into a brand new life. Six months later, my mom was also healed when she received a word of knowledge while watching the 700 Club. A few days before her healing, she had asked me to give her my opinion about a show she had just started watching. I have to be honest, although I enjoyed the testimonies; I thought the show was sort of fake. But a few days later when Mom had once again asked me to watch it with her, I quickly changed my opinion.

Near the end of the show, a word of knowledge was given that God was healing someone. I honestly can't tell you what the word said because mom had a death grip on my hand and was telling me to pray for the person who had been mentioned. "Jeannie we must pray for this person!" Mom stated in a serious tone, "I can feel this prayer. It must be someone close to me."

Since I had never heard of a word of knowledge before, the situation was uncomfortable for me. But I followed along just to humor her. Then everything changed. One second Mom was squeezing my hand, and the next she was jumping up and down yelling, "It's me! It's me! Jesus just healed me!" She then took a mad dash to the freezer, pulled out some left over birthday cake and began to gorge on it before it was even thawed. I remember thinking "Oh no! Mom is going to die!"

Later that night, Mom proved to my father that she had been healed when she accepted his challenge and ate a can of (preservative filled) Vienna sausages in front of him. With each bite he begged her to stop because he didn't want her to be sick all night. After she made it through the night reaction free, Dad agreed with her that she had been healed.

Because of God's grace and mercy, 1986 was the beginning of new lives for both my mom and me. Since we were no longer hindered by immune system disorders, chemical sensitivities, and central nervous system reactions we could live normal lives. I continued to raise my children and minister in the various neighborhoods I lived in. Mom helped Dad run his engineering firm, became involved in ministry opportunities, and even ended up running for the Texas State School Board. She also traveled a lot.

A few years into her illness, when Mom was still confined to her bed, a friend had come over to see her with some suitcases and a word from the Lord. "Frances, her friend boldly stated, "God told me to buy you these suitcases because you are going to travel the world." At the time, even traveling to church was an impossibility. But a few years later, Mom did exactly that. Over the next twenty years Mom and Dad would journey to five different continents. Everywhere Mom went she handed out tracts and introduced people to Jesus, her personal Savior and Healer. As far as I know, Mom never spoke from a pulpit, but I still run into people whose lives were impacted by her love for the Lord and her courageous faith.

In 1986, as I held my mom's hand, God spoke to her circumstances and said, *"It is finished!"* as He healed her and gave her a new life. Almost thirty years later, as Dad held Mom's hand, God spoke to her spirit and said *"It is finished. Come join me in eternal life."*

♥ *Heart Encounter* ♥

1. God sees the beginning from the end. He once spoke to me in the midst of a difficult trial, *"I know the length and breadth of this trial, and I know exactly what I am going to bring out of it."* When you are suffering, does it comfort you to know that God knows both the beginning and the end?

2. Although Mom wasn't healed the day her friend showed up with the suitcases, I believe that in heaven God had declared that her trial was finished. Do you believe that our prayers are often answered in the heavenlies before we see them answered on earth?

3. Once when I was suffering from a neck injury, the Lord spoke to my heart, *"I have healed you."* Although I didn't experience the physical manifestation of my healing for a few more months, the day He spoke it I knew I was healed. Has God

spoken healing over an area in your life that you have yet to see come to pass?

4. The Bible tells us in Isaiah 53:5 "But He *was* wounded for our transgressions, *He was* bruised for our iniquities; The chastisement for our peace *was* upon Him; And by His stripes we are healed." Even though many times I have received personal healing and have had the privilege of seeing God heal many of my family and friends, there have also been times when I have not seen the manifestation of physical healing this side of heaven. In those times, I have to remember that Jesus also took upon Himself the chastisement for our peace. I think it's always right to pray and believe for healing, but we also need to rest in the peace that God's presence brings, even when we don't understand certain outcomes. Can you think of an instance when you experienced God's healing for you or someone you know? Have there been times when you didn't see the healing you prayed for?

When Jesus was dying on the cross, I believe that He knew everyone who would ever live. When He declared, "It is finished" He saw you and me. The old religion was finished (brought to completion) and the new (relationship) had begun. He knew exactly when you and

I would be born, and He knew our purposes. As the blood poured from his head, hands, and feet, He stood in the gap for us and released His promises in our lives.

In 1986, when God touched our physical bodies, my mother and I began to take hold of more of those promises. Are there some spiritual, emotional, and physical promises that you need to take hold of? Jesus is reaching out to you and saying, "It is finished." Will you reach out and grab God's hand and receive all He has for you?

Let's Pray:

Precious Lord, thank you for finishing everything for me on Calvary. Your mercies are new every morning and great is your faithfulness. I take hold of your promises and receive all that you have for me. Thank you for being my healer. Heal my mind, my soul, and my body, In Jesus name...Amen

Reflections:

_____
_____
_____
_____
_____
_____
_____
_____
_____

Let Me Be God!

$\mathcal{A}$s 2009 was coming to a close, nothing seemed to be making sense. It started back in October of 2009, when I was signing up to work extra days to cover for fellow employees who wanted to take holiday vacations. I wrote my name next to a few days in November and early December. When I started to sign next to December 19th, the Lord spoke to my heart: *"Don't work the 19th. I have a surprise for you."*

"Hmmm—maybe I'll meet Mr. Tall, Dark, and Handsome," I mused.

My youngest daughter Rebekah, who was living in Twentynine Palms, California at the time, was expecting my first grandson on the 29th of December. So I was planning to take my vacation beginning the 22nd. But when it came time to schedule my vacation, I felt to change my plans and ask for my vacation time for the first week of January. I assumed that meant the baby would be late.

A week later, when I noticed that no one had signed up to work the 19th yet, I once again thought about working it. "Since the baby probably won't be born until January," I rationalized, "maybe I should just forfeit my surprise from the Lord and work December 19th anyway. Besides, I need the extra money." But when I reached for my pen, I heard in my spirit, *"Let me be God!"* It was a statement that would become very familiar to me during the next few months.

"Let me be God!" reminded me that I wasn't in control when my oldest daughter announced that she had scheduled a later flight and would not be home for Christmas. *"Let me be God!"* helped me to let go when my youngest son announced he was leaving town for the holidays. And *"Let me be God!"* calmed me each time my daughter Rebekah called to let me know that she *really* wanted me there for the birth of the baby. *"Let me be God!"* also reminded me that God was my provider whenever I wondered how I would obtain the gas money for our trip to California in January.

Although I had often thought about my *surprise* throughout the month of October and the first part of November, in the midst of all the busyness and changed plans, by the time December rolled around, I had completely forgotten about it. That is, until Thursday evening, the 17th when Rebekah called saying that her "false labor" was becoming more regular, making her wonder if it was really false.

I told Rebekah that I would be praying and reminded her to keep me informed. Then I called some of my friends to pray as well. When I shared the news with my friend Kannesa, and told her that I wasn't going to be present for the birth of the baby, she was troubled. "Are you sure there is no way for you to go?" she questioned. I told her that I was disappointed, but since I had surrendered my concerns considering my children, I was just "trusting." Besides, every time I prayed for direction, I didn't get any answers except *"Let me be God!"*

To make a long story short, the following afternoon, Rebekah was in the hospital in labor. I had been blessed with my employee Christmas check early and was heading to California with my dedicated friend Kannesa in the driver's seat. My son, his girlfriend and my daughter's best friend were crammed in the back. About an hour from Twentynine Palms, I received a text from my son-in-law telling me that the baby had been born. I anxiously awaited a second text with more details, but none came. It seemed like an eternity before my phone alerted me another text had arrived. *Something's wrong. The baby's having difficulty breathing and is being transported to Palm Springs.* We changed course in direction. As I rapidly shot texts across the nation for prayer, God's peace enveloped me as He once again reminded me, *"Let me be God!"*

Rebekah had the hospital in Twentynine Palms release her a couple of hours after delivery so she could be with her baby. She and her husband were still en route to Palm Springs when our little entourage arrived at the hospital a little after midnight. A few minutes later, I was sitting in the Palm Springs NICU touching and singing to my beautiful new grandson Rhett Tacoma.

Baby Rhett was hooked up to a heart monitor, but he was breathing on his own. As I looked into the angelic face of my grandbaby, God again reminded me of my promised *surprise on the 19th.* My heart overflowed with joy as I thought to myself: "Wow! Lord, I couldn't have thought up anything better!"

After our whirlwind trip to and from Palm Springs, I ended up working a lot of extra hours due to some unforeseen staff emergencies. Little Rhett's hospital stay was extended two weeks for observation purposes. I returned to California on the 2nd of January, just a couple of days after he was released from the hospital.

One morning, while sitting in my daughter and son-in-law's living room with my children, including my oldest daughter who had been led to change her flight until the end of December, and my new grandson, I began to replay the events of the past couple of weeks in my mind. As I reflected on how the scheduling changes, the unforeseen challenges that had arisen, and the supply of finances for two trips instead of one had all come together in such an incredible way, a sense of awe began to rise up in my spirit. "Wow, Lord!" I inwardly expressed. I can't believe how you put everything together! "I'm so glad that *You* are God and *I* am not!"

♥ *Heart Encounter* ♥

1. One of my favorite scriptures is Proverbs 3:5-6. I have learned that when I release things I don't understand and trust God to put them together, I am often amazed at how *He* does it! Can you relate? Give an example.

2. Maybe there is a situation in your life right now where your "plans" have been changed. How does what you actually see happening differ from what you had planned?

3. I love the way Joseph and Mary "leaned not on their own understanding" and trusted. I'm sure when they thought about the delivery of their baby they weren't picturing, Bethlehem, a manger, and smelly animals. (Luke Chapter 2) But as some doors were closed, others opened and God showed himself to be God in miraculous ways!

4. How can the circumstances surrounding the birth of Jesus encourage you in your current circumstances?

This morning I had a situation arise with a family member. I immediately wanted to jump in and "fix" everything. Once again, I heard my Heavenly Father's voice reminding me to let *Him* be God. Maybe you are going through a season in your life that you don't understand. Maybe you have tried to no avail to do all *you* can do to make things work out the way *you planned* (I used to be an expert at that). If so, may I encourage you to *let go* of the reins and just *Let God be God.* Not only does *He* do an awfully good job, but in the process, He is often full of surprises!

Let's Pray:

Heavenly Father, I'm so thankful that you are God, and I'm not. You see the beginning from the end, when I can't see past this minute. Help me to trust you and "lean not upon my own understanding" as you change my plans and "redirect my paths." Thank you for being loving, faithful, and merciful. Thank you also for the wonderful surprises that are awaiting me. Precious Lord, I choose to rest in your care and *Let you be God!* In Jesus' Name...Amen!

Reflections:

_____

_____

_____

_____

_____

_____

_____

_____

_____

Unseen Ears

When my children were young, my friends and I often exchanged "baby stories." Before you think, "how sweet," let me inform you that some of these sharing sessions sounded more like America's Most Wanted for infants than recounts of pregnancies, deliveries, and baby's first few months home. One day when it was my turn to "share," I told the story of my first born. It went something like this:

During my first trimester I was so sick I was bedridden most of the time. I had to eat organic steaks because the doctor said keeping down organic meat for at least ten minutes would enable me to get some nutrients. Although my ten-minute gorge and puke meal sessions kept me from starving, I still lost twenty pounds. I managed to gain most of it back during my last trimester, but my friends affectionately told me that my pregnant figure resembled that of a toothpick stuck through an olive.

When it was time for my son's birth I was graced with 24 hours of back labor because he was in a post-faced position. Since my contractions weren't setting up, I was eventually administered a drug to help me dilate. Although the medication caused my contractions to be more painful and intense, I refused painkillers because of my history of extreme allergic reactions.

Thankfully, when my baby boy Joshua finally decided to make his appearance, he was both beautiful and healthy. But after we brought him home from the hospital, he developed jaundice. He was also colicky. Laying him in the sun during the day as the doctor instructed helped his jaundice, but nothing seemed to relieve his colic.

Joshua would start screaming around 6 o'clock every evening and wouldn't fall asleep until 3 or 4 in the morning. When colic medications, home remedies, and various colic holds didn't work, Joshua's pediatrician suggested that he might sleep some at night if he stayed awake all day. "Keep the baby active—even if you have to turn him upside down," instructed the doctor. I tried. I played with his hands, tickled his feet, assisted him in doing baby sit-ups, and tipped him upside down during regular intervals. Occasionally, one eye would squint halfway open, but then almost immediately shut again. The only thing left to do would have been to hang him upside down in the closet by his toes. But fears of a CPS visit and/or years of therapy in order to convince him he wasn't an opossum stopped me.

Night after night, I sat in the living room of our little one bedroom apartment, rocking and jiggling Joshua, trying to keep him quiet so as not to awaken and upset my husband Joe. I begged, pleaded, and prayed, and eventually broke down and cried right along with my son. After a couple of weeks I succumbed to total physical, emotional, and mental exhaustion.

As I continued to explain the frustration of trying to find a solution to the colic to my neighbor (which by the way, since I was breastfeeding, eliminating milk from my diet helped), I felt a tug on my shirt. I peered down into the face of my adorable blonde-headed now five-year old, Joshua. His slightly watery green eyes looked up at me as he commented, "Mommy, I'm sorry I was such a bad baby." My heart sank. I bent down on one knee, looked him straight in the face and said, "Sweetie, you weren't a bad baby; you were just a sick baby."

Later that afternoon, as I held Joshua and told him of the blessing that he was to me, I began to wonder how many other times I had said things whether knowingly or unknowingly that had wounded my children. How many times had I been insensitive to their little spirits when I was talking about them to others, or when I was venting openly to them in my frustration and anger? How many times in watching my facial expressions and hearing my careless words were my precious children hearing and perceiving that something was *wrong* with them? I'm afraid the answer was "way too many."

The other day, as I read the rough draft of this story

to my friend Lisa, I was challenged to think about other careless words that I have spoken. Lisa mentioned that God had been convicting her of how she had talked about her pregnancies. Apparently, she had gained a lot of weight when she was pregnant with her daughter. Recently, her daughter had told her, "Mommy, I'm sorry I made you fat." Lisa said that not only had the Holy Spirit convicted her about what she said in front of her daughter, she was also encouraged to think positively about her pregnancy experiences.

Lisa's words caused me to examine my own heart and negativity concerning my pregnancies. So I asked the Lord to show me how *He* saw my pregnancies. I was amazed at all He brought to mind! My pregnancy with my first born was a time of miracles. During my first trimester, when the doctor thought I was going to miscarry, I heard God speak to my spirit, *"The baby is a boy. His name is Joshua, and I have called him to be a leader."* Joshua has now been in leadership for many years.

Being stuck in bed, I constantly read my Bible and prayed. Since I was unable to take care of myself, I was deeply troubled. How would I care for a baby? When I was five months pregnant with Joshua, I had a series of dreams about certain scriptures. Shortly afterwards, I called some friends who had been praying for me. They took me to their Bible study where I was anointed with oil and prayed for. God miraculously touched me and I was healed of my central nervous system reactions, headaches, and even a painful knee injury.

As I thought about my other pregnancies, similar words of life came to the forefront of my mind. With each pregnancy I learned more about the Lord, His provision, and His value of life. I learned that there are no such things as mistakes when it comes to conception and that all life is precious, no matter what lies the enemy tried to tell me in my own mind or through the words of others. (It was amazing after I had my third child, how many people felt that they had a responsibility to inform me that I had gone over my allotted 2.5 children. I still wonder what a .5 child looks like.) I also learned that God is faithful, and that He is perfectly capable to care for our children and for us.

The Bible tells us in Proverbs 18:21 that "Death and life *are* in the power of the tongue: And those who love it will eat its fruit." It is powerful to *speak life* over our children, during every season, beginning in the womb. If you don't have children, you can *speak life* over the children within your sphere of influence.

Research has shown that memories begin when a child is in utero. If you have not already taken the opportunity to do so, began now to speak value, purpose, and blessing over your children. As you thank the Lord for the precious gifts He has given you, you might also want to ask Him to give you insight, if applicable, concerning your pregnancies.

None of us are perfect (believe me I have blown it many times.) But, through the years, I have learned that children's spirits can easily be wounded by careless words. That is why I try to be more sensitive to my children's and (now grandchildren's) feelings, even if it means biting my tongue and praying before I speak. Our wonderful Father God speaks love and identity to us. Let's pass the blessing on to those we love.

♥ *Heart Encounter* ♥

1. What words were spoken about you or to you when you were growing up?

2. How did those words, good or bad, affect your self-image?

3. How did they affect your view of others?

4. As I have mentioned previously, Psalm 127:3 tells us "Behold children *are* a heritage from the Lord, the fruit of the womb *is* a reward." As you were growing up did you feel like you were a reward? Why or why not?

5. Unfortunately, many parents are either too broken themselves, or they just don't possess the understanding to bless their children. Because I was raised hearing a lot of condemnation from some of the people in my sphere of influence, I continued the pattern with my own children. Reading a book combining *The Blessing* and *The Gift of Honor*, both by Gary Smalley and John Trent, revolutionized the way that I not only saw my children, but the way that I spoke to them as well. Have you ever had someone speak a blessing over you?

6. If not, ask the Lord to give you His words of blessing. You can also have a blessing spoken over you by a parent, pastor, or close friend. Are you are ready to receive a blessing?

7. It is important to bless our children, but it is equally important that you and I bless all of God's children, including adults. Think of a few people who need encouragement or validation. What are some words of life you can say to them to bless them?

Speaking blessing is so powerful it can change the course of someone's life! I recently heard a pastor share a heart-breaking incident that took place at a pastors' convention. The speaker shared how not receiving his parent's blessing had brought him much heart ache and confusion. He then asked all present to come forward if they had never bccn blessed by their parents, especially their fathers. Over half of the pastors came forward.

In Genesis chapter 26, when Jacob takes advantage of his brother Esau and easily manipulates him to sell his inheritance for a simple meal of pottage and bread, Esau doesn't seem too concerned. But in chapter 27, when Jacob steals Esau's blessing, Esau weeps out loud. The loss of the things probably aggravated Esau, but the loss of the blessing devastated him. Should you and I ignore something so full of life? May we always remember to exercise the *power of our tongues* and bless the ones we love!

Let's Pray:

Dear Lord, forgive me for saying things that have grieved the hearts of my children or the children around me. Bring me revelation concerning my/others pregnancies and/or deliveries. Remind me of what an incredible blessing it is to be a parent (or spiritual parent). Help me to speak *life* over my children or over the children in my life, in every season of their growth. I thank you that you are my parent who speaks blessing over me. Help me be the parent who passes that blessing on to my treasures in this life—my children.

It's wonderful and necessary to give the blessing, but it is also vital to receive the blessing. Whether or not you ever received the blessing as a child, I would encourage you to place *your* name in the blanks below, as you read the following paragraph—and be blessed!

Lord, Thank you for _____. What a wonderful treasure _____ is! Lord, thank you for forming and fashioning _____ in _____'s mother's womb. Thank you for blessing _____ with talents and abilities specifically chosen for _____. Lord, I bless _____'s future. May your love and truth be poured out over _____'s life. May _____ prosper in body, soul, and spirit, and may _____ daily grow in

39

_____'s understanding of your unfathomable love for _____. I declare_____ to be cherished, chosen, and blessed! In Jesus' Name…Amen!

Reflections:

_____

_____

_____

_____

_____

_____

_____

_____

_____

S.O.S.

$\mathcal{D}$ad! Mom! Princess had her puppies! Can we keep them? Pleeeeeease?" The anxious chorus echoed throughout the house as my five siblings and I ecstatically bounded toward the back door after a peek through a bedroom window revealed the long awaited early morning discovery. In no time at all, we were gathered around in a semi-circle marveling at the miracle of new life before us. A mixture of delight and awe filled our young minds as we observed the mass of tiny bodies, heads, tails, and paws that seemed to move as a single organism while each puppy tried to claim its place of nourishment.

Although we were all excited as visions of playing with frolicking puppies danced through our little heads, my younger brother and I treasured a secret joy because now it was finally *our* turn! You see, in our family there was a tradition that anytime there were new baby anythings: puppies, kittens, gerbils etc., a claim was staked. Since whoever, in descending order, didn't have the "last pet" got first rites to the new litter, my younger brother David and I were to each have a puppy of our very own.

As soon as the "oohs' and "ahhs" subsided, David and I moved in to lay hold of what was rightfully ours. I carefully selected a small brown and white puppy, which I decidedly named "Muttskins," because I thought the name carried a certain comical tone as well as it being both logical and fitting. After all, he was a mutt and he did have skin.

David didn't see a puppy that would suit him so he begged Dad and Mom to let him have one from his best friend's dog's litter. He named his puppy, which was similar in color but larger in size, "S.O.S". Apparently, he had become mesmerized by the abnormally large paws that the puppy was sporting and saw visions of a hero.

My brother David had a little bit of a temper, so whenever he was bullied at school, he refused to back down. As a result he was consistently getting into fights. Being of smaller stature in his younger years, he would get…how do you say it…CLOBBERED! Thus, when he first laid eyes on S.O.S.'s big feet, immediately, the wheels began to turn in his little head. Big paws…Big Boys…BIGGER DOG! YEAH! I'm RESCUED!

From that day forward I winced at each new stage of growth in Muttskins. If I had had it my way, he would have stayed little forever. David, on the other hand, couldn't wait for S.O.S to grow into his paws. I think he even fed him extra food when no one was looking to help him quickly gain as much weight as possible.

As the weeks went by, David would share his marvelous plot with anyone who was willing to lend him an ear. When he would get to the part about S.O.S. he could hardly contain his excitement. With great enthusiasm, he would gesture wildly, his arms flailing in all directions, as he explained a future encounter with one of his foes. He had it planned to a T how when being challenged by a bully he had planned to cup his hands to his mouth and send out a cry of alarm "S.O.S.!" And about how upon hearing his name, David's beloved pet— his hero—instinctively knowing his master was in trouble, would hurl his monstrous frame into the air and come barreling over the fence, ferociously sending his attacker running for his life.

With each passing month, David's dreams of salvation escalated as S.O.S.'s paws continued to grow. But, in time, his hopes began to fade as it became obvious to all that the dog's paws were the only things on him still growing. It wasn't long before David's dog, his rescuer, his hero, who would leap the fence in a single bound, became the butt of my family's jokes. For you see, S.O.S. ended up being nothing but a short dog with very large paws!

How many times do you and I dream of a hero—a rescuer—someone who will come in and save the day? Or maybe our rescuer isn't a person at all. Maybe it is *something*, or *sometime*, or a position we are waiting for. Maybe it is an "if only." If only I could get this car, this house, this job, this degree, or this promotion, etc. If only I could get married, go on vacation, win the lottery, or just start over. If only I could just_____ (fill in the blank) then I would no longer be tormented, life would be easier, and I would be happy. Although these thoughts sound promising, since you and I were never intended to make people our saviors or put our faith in temporal things, the opposite rings true. And like my brother with S.O.S., we will end up disillusioned once we discover we were putting our faith in nothing but a little dog with big feet.

♥ *Heart Encounter* ♥

1. Who or what are some of the bullies you face?

2. Are you waiting to be rescued? Where are you putting your hope?

3. There is an old hymn that I just love. I find myself singing it often when I'm facing life's bullies. Here are some of the words: "My hope is built on nothing less than Jesus' blood and righteousness; I dare not

trust the sweetest frame, but wholly lean on Jesus' name. On Christ, the solid rock I stand; all other ground is sinking sand." Aren't those incredible words? How could you apply them to your situation?

4. In 2 Chronicles we read about the life of King Asa. On two separate occasions, Asa is bullied. In 2 Chronicles 14:8-15, who were Asa's bullies?

5. When his enemies came against him, where did Asa put his trust? What was the result of his decision?

6. The Bible tells us in Psalms 20:7 that "some *trust* in chariots, and some in horses; But we will remember the name of the Lord our God." Whose name comes to your mind first when you face life's bullies?

7. Do you believe that placing your hope in God will ultimately bring victory? Explain.

8. Read 2 Chronicles 16:1-9. Where did Asa put his trust this time?

9. Although, in the past, Asa had seen God miraculously deliver his army from the Ethiopians, this time he chose to trust in man. What were the consequences of his decision?

10. Have you ever experienced God "come through for you," but the next time a crisis hits, you tried to figure out things on your own? I'm guilty. Although I have seen God miraculously intervene in my life so many times I have lost count, I still have moments when I freak out and try to do things my own way when opposition comes. Psalm 18:2-4 states: "The Lord is my rock and my fortress and my deliverer; My God, my strength, in whom I will trust, My shield and the horn of my salvation, my stronghold. I will call upon the Lord, *who is worthy* to be praised; So shall I be saved from my enemies." I am so thankful that God not only answers when I call, but He also takes action. Are you calling upon Him now? What are you asking of Him?

There is only one Savior and his name is Jesus Christ. Only He, and He alone, can fight the bullies in our lives that torment us—like fear, depression, unworthiness, and addictions—or the bullies that challenge us at our weakest points, like disillusionment and pride. Jesus is the ultimate hero! He conquered our enemies (aka bullies) over 2,000 years ago when He suffered and died in our place on Calvary. If you set your sights on Him and Him alone, He will never come up short on your behalf!

Let's Pray:

Precious Lord, I call upon you as my hero—my rescuer. I place my faith and trust in you. You bore everything on Calvary for me so my bullies would be defeated. Nothing can satisfy me and bring me peace except you and you alone. No other person, place, thing, or position can fulfill me. Come, Sweet Lord! Come and fill the empty places in my life with your hope and your love. Come and chase away the enemies that torment my soul. Bring me freedom and release—My Lord—My God—My Savior—My friend—My HERO!!! In Jesus' Name...Amen!

Reflections:

_____

_____

_____

_____

_____

_____

_____

_____

_____

Super

Some mornings I hit the floor feeling like a warrior princess ready to conquer my enemies. Armed with my Holy Spirit super powers of "I can do all things through Christ who strengthens me," I take off running. Throughout the day I can leap tall obstacles in a single bound and outrun speeding inconveniences. I might even be able to catch a bullet or two of offense or rejection in my teeth.

But then there are those "other" days when I want to hide under my covers and *forget* it's morning. I'm already reaching for my super victim cape before I even get out of bed. And forget about leaping. It's a major accomplishment just to crawl. Instead of rejoicing and singing "This is the Day that the Lord Has Made" and "Your Grace is Enough," I'm inwardly rehearsing, "Woe is me. I'm stuck in this place," and "Lord, I've had enough."

After I slither to the floor repeating, "Lord, you have

got to help me here," I spend a little time begging for strength, and then get up and go about my day. Throughout the day, I crash into obstacles. My patience, or lack thereof, gets run over by every inconvenience, and the bullets of offense and rejection go straight into my heart. I might be standing on the outside, but I'm crippled on the inside by fears, circumstances, disappointments, and past wounds.

Those are the days I remember the crippled man in John 5. The Bible tells us that this man had been wrought with infirmities for 38 years. He lay with the sick, lame, blind, and paralyzed people by a pool called Bethesda. It was believed that once a year an angel stirred the waters of the pool. And the first person who entered the pool, after the angel had stirred the water, would be healed. One day, while he was hanging out on his mat, Jesus showed up. When Jesus saw him lying there he asked the man an interesting question: "Do you want to be made well?" "The sick man answered Him, 'Sir, I have no man to put me into the pool when the water is stirred up; but while I am coming, another steps down before me.' Jesus said to him, 'Rise, take up your bed and walk.' And immediately, the man was made well, took up his bed, and walked" (John 5:7-9).

In a way, I can relate to this story. For many years I was like the infirm man waiting for the waters to be stirred. Although I outwardly participated in this journey we call life, inwardly, I lay on my beggar's mat, abused and broken. I longed to be rescued, but I thought my circumstances had to change for my soul to be healed. "If someone could just help me into the water," I would tell myself, "Then I would be healed." But one day, Jesus showed up and asked me, "Do you *want* to be made well?"

What a question to ask a man who had been paralyzed for 38 years. What a question to ask a 38-year-old woman who had been crippled by hurts, fears, and disappointments—a woman going through a divorce. But Jesus asked it all the same.

The man answered quickly; it took *me* longer. First, I had to believe I *could* be made well, and then I had to accept what being made well would involve. I would have to take up my bed and walk. That meant no more excuses. No more waiting for a rescuer. No more waiting at all.

Being well meant taking action. It meant rising up. It meant I had to leave my familiar place by the waters of the "if only pool" and step into the vast ocean of the unknown. It meant taking on a new identity. It meant more responsibility. It meant facing my past and thinking about my future. It meant stepping into a whole new life. (For me, that new life began with learning that God truly loved me and had my best interests in mind.) It meant trusting Him, even when I didn't understand. It also meant studying and receiving truth concerning my identity and relationships. It meant breaking codependent patterns and taking responsibility for my past, present, and future choices.

During the journey, there were many times I would grab my beggar's mat and go back to the pool. But each time I ran to the familiar, I ran into my Savior. "Do you want to be made well?" He would once again ask me.

And He keeps on asking.

Yes, there might be some mornings when I still grab my super victim cape and get bombarded by frustrations. But I know my Savior is standing before me or even holding my hand. As I look back toward the waters of Bethesda, Jesus looks lovingly into my eyes and asks once again: "Do you want to be made well? Quit looking at the waters in the pool and receive my living water. Let me take you beside the still waters."

In His presence I am refreshed, comforted, encouraged, admonished, challenged, renewed, and restored—giving me the courage to once again rise up, take up my bed, and walk into a NEW DAY…walk into a NEW SEASON…and walk into a NEW LIFE!

♥ *Heart Encounter* ♥

1. Why do you think Jesus asked the crippled man if he wanted to be made well instead of asking him, "Do you believe I can heal you?

2. I love the way Jesus always goes to the heart of the matter! The man's problem wasn't faith. It took a lot of faith for him to believe that he would be healed if he was first in the pool after the stirring of the waters. The man was a beggar for many years. Maybe he feared the responsibility of a normal life, or maybe he was too dependent on others. Maybe he had just flat given up. We don't know why Jesus asked him that question, but I can almost guarantee it exposed what was in his heart. What would stir in your heart if Jesus walked up to you right now and asked you, "Do you want to be made well?"

3. Hurts, disappointments, mostly from abuse, crippled me. Fear and helplessness kept me from getting well. Can you relate? Are there some hurts and disappointments that have crippled you? If so, what are they? What is keeping you from being made well?

4. The Lord led me to the story of the crippled man by the pool of Bethesda to reveal my victim mentality. Although I *wanted* to walk, I was convinced that I couldn't unless someone helped me into the pool (rescued me.) Being asked if I wanted to be made well forced me to reevaluate both my thinking and my past—and sometimes present—actions. Are you

waiting for someone to heal you from hurts and disappointments that have crippled you? Explain.

5. Maybe you are suffering from a victim mentality like I was, and sometimes still do. If so, what steps might you take in order to take up your mat and walk in victory?

A victim says, "I can't unless...," but an overcomer says, "I can do all things through Christ who strengthens me." A victim says, "No one understands me." But an overcomer says, "I don't need to be understood; God knows my heart." A victim says, "I'll never change," but an overcomer says, "God is faithful to complete the good work that He has begun in me." Yes, God knows our hearts. He also knows our hurts, and our disappointments, and our crippling mindsets. And He loves us so much that He wants us to be whole. That is why He still continues to ask us, "Do you want to be made well?" Today, is He asking you if you want to be made well? If so, may you "Rise and take up your bed and walk"—or even run with Him.

Let's Pray:

Dear Lord, thank you for loving me. Reveal any areas in my heart where I may still be crippled. Show me how past hurts and disappointments have affected my present and past decisions. Shine the searchlight of your love in my heart and expose any victim mindsets. Teach me to think and walk as the overcomer you have created me to be. In Jesus' Name…Amen!

Reflections:

_____

_____

_____

_____

_____

_____

_____

_____

_____

Stretch Marks

$\mathcal{A}$ few weeks ago, while consulting with my not-so-friendly bathroom mirror, I discovered that parts of my anatomy have fallen with gravity and time. Unfortunately, it doesn't look like they will be getting back up—at least, not in this lifetime. What makes matters worse is that a roadmap of "stretch marks" has been left to confirm their shift in direction.

Stretch marks—nobody wants them, but most women have them. Although we often think of the negative aspect of stretch marks—unwanted weight, looser skin, etc.—it's also important to think of them positively. A while back, as I was talking to a friend about how God loves to stretch us, she piped up, "That's right, and I have the stretch marks to prove it!"

That night, I began to think of stretch marks in relation to my pregnancies. The stretch marks which began to appear during my second trimester, not only signified life, they also signified growth. And although I didn't much care for the signal, each new mark held great significance, reflecting a veiled beauty all its own.

Upon entering my last trimester, there were times when I would toss and turn all night. Upon awakening the next morning, I would discover that not only had my belly increased in size, it had also increased in pattern. It was obvious that I was being stretched, and it didn't feel good. It also rarely *feels good*, when we are being stretched in order to contain the new life that God is developing in us.

The other day after I read an e-mail from a friend who was getting ready to go on a mission trip to Africa, I looked down and noticed a rubber band sitting near the edge of my desk. I thought to myself, "Boy, is she going to be stretched!" As I picked up the rubber band and drew it back, the realization hit me that the more I pulled, the farther it would fly. The Holy Spirit then began to minister to my heart that the extent we allow the Lord to stretch us is the extent that we will be released into our purpose and destiny.

The next day, my youngest son Caleb and I were having an in depth discussion. When I brought up the analogy of the rubber band he asked, "Mom, are you talking about shooting it normally or scientifically?" Since the blank look that registered on my face immediately cued him in on the fact that I didn't have a clue what he was talking about, he began to tell me about an example he had seen at a Creation Seminar.

"When a rubber band is pulled straight back in a

normal fashion, each side is equally stretched, which causes the two sides to conflict and vibrate against each other as it flies through the air—causing resistance and limiting its flight," Caleb explained. "The scientific way eliminates the conflict by making just one little adjustment. Instead of pulling straight back and tightening both sides evenly, you must pull a little off center stretching one side closer to you, causing it to have more tension than the other. This slight shift makes all of the difference in the rubber band's flying to its full potential, because it causes the rubber band to move in a circular motion, eliminating the friction between the two sides."

As my son was explaining the contrast, he shared, "Mom, that's how it is with our walk with the Lord. When we are not in the Word and seeking after God, our flesh and spirit will constantly conflict as we move forward. But if our hearts are toward God, it's like shooting a rubber band the scientific way. The side that is stretched the most (our spirits) will lead causing the other (the flesh) to follow. Eliminating the conflict between our flesh and spirit enables us to reach our full potential as we are released into our purpose."

Wow! I sat there open-mouthed as I drank in the divine inspiration God was pouring in and through my son. I could definitely feel the band being pulled toward my heart. "Yes, Lord," I inwardly voiced, "Stretch me and release me into the purpose you have planned for me—but do it scientifically."

♥ *Heart Encounter* ♥

1. Can you think of times is your life when you have been stretched in order to facilitate growth? Are you being stretched now? Explain.

2. I am sure that there are more times than I can remember when God has had to stretch me in order to take me forward. Read Genesis 12. Do you believe that when God called Abram to leave all he knew and go to an unknown land, he understood and/or was comfortable with the instructions? Would you have been?

3. There have been times in my life when God has totally busted open the "boxes" in which I have put Him. Thinking God worked in only ways I understood gave me a sense of security and control. I can't even imagine the "God boxes" that were being broken in Abram's understanding, as well as the comfort zones that were shattered! He didn't even know where he was going! Have you ever found yourself challenged like Abram to go forward without knowing the outcome? If so, as you went forward, what were some of the "God boxes" that were broken in your life?

Were your comfort zones also shattered in the process? Explain.

4. What were some of the results of Abram being stretched? What have been some of the results of you being stretched?

5. God rocking Abram's world ultimately brought him to inherit his promises and move into his destiny. Do you believe that Abram could have fulfilled his full potential if he had stayed in his comfort zone? Do you believe you will fulfill yours if you stay where you are now? Why or why not?

6. As Abram changed, the Lord left stretch marks on Abram's life, one of them being his new name of "Abraham." As God changes us He might not give us a new name, but He does give us a new identity. What are some of the evidences you bear to denote the changes in you?

7. As I mentioned earlier, God loves to grow us. As He forms us more into the image of His Son, we have to do away with some of the *old* in order to make room for the *new*. Read about the illustration of the wine

skins in Matthew 9:17. When we rely on ourselves or our own understanding, we are like the old wine skins that become brittle and break when they are expanded. But when we rely on Jesus, we become new containers that easily expand to contain *new* wine. Are you ready to be filled?

Last week, the Lord spoke to my heart that He was not as concerned about my comfort as He was my calling. A few days later I turned on the TV and heard a well known speaker say the same thing. I think God is trying to tell me something here! Stretching breaks our comfort zones, releases us toward our destinies, and leaves marks of change in our hearts and on our lives. When you and I are pulled towards the heart of God as we are stretched, we will be released to reach our full potential. And similar to Abraham, we not only will bear the marks that signify the beauty of our growth, but we will also leave a map that will give direction to those who are following after us. So tell me—Are you ready to be **S-T-R-E-T-C-H-E-D?**

Let's Pray:

Dear Lord, thank you for always growing me. I choose to be like a rubber band that flies to its full potential. I know, because of your love, you will not stretch me until I break and am destroyed; instead you will only pull me as taut as necessary to shoot me forward. I am thankful that your heart is for me, and that you draw me close in the process of breaking my comfort zones and expanding me to receive more of you. Thank you for the marks that forever signify the change. I know that you understand *stretch marks* because your body was bruised and beaten for my healing and freedom. Thank you, Jesus, for making the ultimate stretch when you opened your arms to all mankind in a final gesture of love and laid down your life. In Jesus' Name...Amen!

Reflections:

_____
_____
_____
_____
_____
_____
_____
_____

The Doll

*A*s I carefully folded the decorative paper over the last edge of the box to disguise my latest purchase, I couldn't help but smile at the thought of what lay hidden inside. Earlier in the day I had spied her sitting near the edge of the shelf in the clearance section of our local department store. Her dainty dress, ornamented with ribbons and bows, had caught my eye, but her delicate features were what had tugged at my heart. She had chestnut brown hair, which encircled a beautiful face, accentuated by a lovely pair of brown eyes, rosy cheeks, and a pleasant little mouth that curved upward to form a simple smile. To add to my pleasure, there was a small turnkey on her back, that when wound, played a delightful tune as her small frame seemingly came to life, causing her gently bent arms to raise up and down as she pivoted from her tiny waist. As I stood there admiring her, I just knew that I had to buy her for my youngest daughter. She would absolutely adore this porcelain doll!

My purchase being made, I had rushed home, locked myself in my room, and immediately applied myself to the task of preparing and concealing the secret gift. And now, securely wrapped, labeled, and decorated with ribbons and a red bow, she was ready to be hidden away—for a season. As I gently placed the box on the top shelf of the closet, a few musical notes were released. "Shhh!" I thought to myself, "you will give yourself away!" Then I quickly covered the gift with some miscellaneous items within my grasp and quietly closed the closet door.

With the relief of not being discovered, I sat down on the edge of my bed, momentarily taken far away from the sorrow of my current season. I was enjoying a day to come. My daughter's tenth birthday was still months away, but I could envision it as if it were tomorrow. I could see the light dance in her eyes as she peeled back the packaging. I could anticipate her hands clapping ecstatically as she lifted the doll from the box, and I could hear her shrill squeal of delight as she discovered the key that released the charming melody, all the while her countenance reflecting the joy in her heart as she marveled at the beauty of the gift that lay before her. I could hardly wait!

During the months that followed, from time to time, my daughter would drop hints (in not so subtle ways) as to what she would want for her birthday. And with each suggestion I would smile at her in response as my mind recollected the beautiful doll tucked away in obscurity behind the items on my shelf. Although with the passing of each day it became harder to wait, I knew that it was necessary. If the gift was not given at just the right time, on just the right day, the full impact of the blessing would be tainted. One day before would be too early; one day afterward, too late. It had to be given at just the right moment for the celebration to be complete. The party would be prepared and *then* the gift would be presented.

One day, as I was mentally organizing the details of the upcoming event, the Lord spoke to my heart, *"Jeannie, do you know the doll that you have hidden away in your closet for your daughter? She doesn't know that it is there, but you do. Just as you are anxiously awaiting the day that you will bless her, I am anxiously awaiting the day that I will bless you."*

During the next few minutes the Lord continued to impress upon my heart that He loves to bless us. After all, it is His nature to bless His children. He then shared with me that He knew the loss I was going through, He felt my grief, and that He too was excited for the day when He would be able to give me my heart's desires that He had hidden away for me. These were precious gifts that were already purchased by His blood, wrapped in His love, and tucked away, waiting for just the right moment to be presented to me—not one day too early— or one day too late, but in His perfect timing, so as not to taint the full impact of the blessing!

♥ *Heart Encounter* ♥

1. Do you believe that God has blessings tucked away especially for you?

2. I believe that we would be absolutely overwhelmed if we could get a glimpse of all of the wonderful things that God has in store for us. The question is: are we willing to trust Him for His timing? I often struggle when it comes to trusting God for His timing. How about you? Do you ever find it hard to trust God's timing? Why or why not?

3. We see the element of God's timing throughout the scriptures. Read Genesis 15:1 through Genesis 18:14. Did Abram and Sarai (In Chapter 17 God changes their names to Abraham and Sarah) believe that God had a blessing for them? Did they trust God's timing? What resulted from their impatience?

4. Meditate on Genesis 18:14: "Is anything too hard for the Lord? *At the appointed time* I will return to you, *according to the time of life*, and Sarah shall

have a son" (italics mine). If the appointed time is the time of life, what does that tell us about rushing God's timing? Is it possible to bring forth conflict and things of death when we get impatient and do things our own way?

5. Unfortunately, I can think of too many instances in my life when instead of trusting God's timing, like Abram and Sarai, I have jumped ahead and made choices out of fear or impatience. The results of my mistrust definitely did *not* bring forth good things. Have you ever done the same? What were the results?

6. In chapter 11 of the book of John we read about the story of Lazarus. How do you think Mary and Martha, Lazarus's sisters, felt when Jesus delayed going to their sick brother?

7. There will be situations in our own lives, as in the death of Lazarus, when God's timing will not make sense. Sometimes, while we are waiting, God will allow things in our lives to die; (i.e. dreams, goals, relationships, etc.) It is often during those times that we feel forgotten or abandoned. Have you ever felt forgotten or abandoned by God

when He didn't seem to come through soon enough? What was the situation?

8. Whether we realize it or not, there is always a reason. Sometimes God will resurrect the very thing that died, but at other times He will just resurrect something in us. Has God ever resurrected a hopeless situation in your life or resurrected something in your heart in the midst? What was resurrected?

9. Look closely at Jesus' reply in John 11:4 when He was informed of Lazarus's illness. "This sickness is not to end in death; but [on the contrary] it is to honor God *and* to promote His glory, that the Son of God may be glorified through (by) it" (AMP). Do you believe that God would have been glorified more if Lazarus had been healed from his illness? What was the result of him being raised from the dead?

10. Verse 45 of John 11 reads that *many believed* as a result. What do you think that celebration looked like?

11. Realizing that God's perfect timing results in the promotion of God's glory and the glorification of Jesus should give us all hope. How does knowing this encourage you as you wait?

My daughter's reaction to her gift was just as I had anticipated. I'm not sure who was blessed more, she or I. Just as I enjoyed blessing my daughter, our Daddy God loves to bless us. But as we go through the twists and turns of this life, it's often hard for us to trust and wait. When we get impatient, we must remember that a gift given out of season would take away from the full impact of the celebration. For even though it might not always seem like it, God's timing is, and always will be, *perfect*!

Let's Pray:

Precious Lord, you are good and you have good gifts for me. Help me to trust your timing. I often get impatient and try to make things happen on my own. Help me not to lean upon my own understanding, making decisions out of impatience or fear. But instead, let me rest in you, knowing that not only do you give good gifts, but you also know the best time in which to give them. In Jesus' Name…Amen!

Reflections:

_____
_____
_____
_____
_____
_____
_____
_____
_____

Something Special For Everyone

*W*hen we named our first puppy "Faith," I had no idea that *my* faith, as well as my patience, was going to be challenged—or better yet—cultivated. Our "little Faith" was a Welsh Springer Spaniel who should have been daily drugged with a large dose of puppy downers. She reminded me of Odie in the "Garfield' comic strips as she bounced around the house with her tongue hanging out and a perpetual dopey grin plastered on her face, leaving slobbery deposits everywhere she went.

Faith was both hyperactive and destructive. Although we bought her puppy chew toys and rawhide bones, she remained loyal to her previous teething preferences—her favorite being the Rattan furniture in the living room. I never knew what carnage I would discover when I woke up every morning. The list of causalities continued to grow—shoes, dolls, army men, my curling iron cord, tape recorder, etc. I feared that we would have to take out a loan before Faith's adult incisors came in.

Our little Faith was also quite social. She spent her early nights (and I mean every one of them) howling at the top of her lungs for company. Since I was the only adult home at night, it was up to me to try to keep her quiet, which was no easy chore. Not only was I tired and hormonal from being pregnant, but the lack of sleep from the continual nightly ruckus had me constantly on edge.

Since Faith hated any kind of restraint, taking her for walks was a character-building experience in itself, and one at which I often failed. Anytime I gave into the pleadings of my children and let one of them help walk her, Faith continuously yanked on her leash until she ended up walking them instead. (Actually dragging would be a more accurate description.) While possessing strength deceptively beyond her small frame, she would invariably yank the handle from the child's hand and take off, leash and all, quickly disappearing out of sight as I futilely yelled after her, "If the pound picks you up, I'm not bailing you out!" And I *meant* it!

The first time Faith bolted and disappeared I thought, "Yeah! She's gone!" But to my chagrin, our little Faith had been blessed with a built-in homing device. When we returned to the house she was sitting on the front porch, slobbering, her dopey grin awaiting our arrival.

Looking back, I think my intense dislike toward Faith had more to do with my marriage than with our dog. My frustration with Faith illuminated the elephant in the room—an elephant that neither my husband Joe nor I had the understanding or willingness to confront at that time. Joe and I were both wounded people who had never dealt with our pasts. He was rarely affectionate to our children or to me. He was also seldom home. I didn't understand boundaries and he wanted to be married in name while continuing to live the lifestyle of a single person. Together we created a mess.

So when Faith came onto the scene, underlying issues quickly surfaced. When Joe would come home, he would make a bee-line for Faith, and then spend hours playing with her, snuggling with her, and rubbing her ears or tummy. It infuriated me to no end to see Faith constantly getting the attention and affection the children and I so desperately longed for.

Because of all Faith's little puppy antics, as well as the attention that was lavished upon her, it was an ongoing battle for me to "have a right heart" toward our obnoxious little dog. And I often questioned as to why I was letting this carefree little canine pull at my emotions.

One night, Faith got really sick. She repeatedly threw up and had bouts of diarrhea. When Joe came home the next morning concern immediately registered on his face. He was positive that Faith had Parvo, a virus that is sometimes lethal for puppies. Since Joe knew someone who recently lost their puppy to Parvo, he didn't give her much of a chance. The bouncy, perky puppy that we knew was not only just still and quiet, she looked almost lifeless. As I sat there staring at little Faith, compassion stirred in me. I didn't want to see her suffer, but I also have to be honest and admit that I wasn't going to miss her much if she failed to recover.

In the midst of feeling guilty while hoping for some relief, I heard the Lord speak to my heart, *"Pray for Faith to be healed."* My immediate response was, "Say what?" I definitely believed that God healed people, but the idea of Him wanting to heal a dog was a little *out there* for me.

I asked my husband if he wanted to pray with me for Faith to get well, and surprisingly, he said, "Yes." So our little family gathered around the sick little puppy and brought her before the Lord believing for her healing. Incredibly, Faith quit throwing up and having diarrhea, and within a couple of hours, she was back to her perky little obnoxious self.

You are probably thinking that after God touched Faith, I fell in love with her, but that was not exactly the case. Although I did lay down the envy in my heart, Faith continued to be a royal "pain in the neck" until she had a litter of puppies. Then she became mellow and tired, like most mothers.

The afternoon we prayed for our puppy Faith, God granted my husband and our children the desires of their hearts. God also increased my faith and taught me a valuable lesson—that He knows our hearts. As God was touching Faith's little body, He touched my bitter heart and taught me that in every situation *He has something special for everyone.*

♥ *Heart Encounter* ♥

1. During the time of my life about which this story was written, I was bound by many lies. I was also very insecure. The fact that I was jealous of a dog, showed that I had a few issues I needed to deal with. But the Lord was both patient and gracious as He used that which "I could understand" to bring revelation to me. I am thankful that God doesn't wait until you and I *get things right* to touch our hearts, our lives, and our circumstances. How about you?

2. I love the fact that the Lord cares so deeply about us that He has something special for everyone in every situation! In the same situation, God might bring conviction to one person and comfort or peace to another. Can you think of a circumstance in your own life where you witnessed God moving in numerous hearts and lives differently? Explain.

3. Another time I witnessed God do *something special for everyone* was when my sister Nancy was diagnosed with an inoperable brain tumor which caused her to be an invalid. While God was drawing her close and teaching her to trust, I was being healed of some buried issues in my life through grieving. At

the same time, my father's faith was growing as he was asking, even strangers, to pray for his daughter. The list could go on and on as each family member and friend experienced God in a new way. Thankfully, the Lord touched Nancy and raised her up. (She and her husband now own a bed and breakfast in AZ.) In Matthew 6:25-34 you and I are encouraged not to worry about what we eat or what we will wear because as our Heavenly Father feeds the birds and clothes the flowers, He will take care of us. If the Lord knows our physical needs, do you not believe that He also knows each and every one of our spiritual and emotional needs as well? Are you or a loved one going through a difficult situation? If so, what are your needs? What are their needs?

4. Throughout the New Testament we have example after example of Jesus meeting people just where they were—the woman at the well, the man with the withered hand, and the man with the legion of demons. The list could go on and on. In every encounter with Christ, each person received exactly what he or she needed. In Philippians 4:19 Paul writes, "And my God shall supply all your needs according to His riches in glory by Christ Jesus." Do you believe that no matter what your situation, Jesus can and will meet you where you are and give you exactly what you need?

Sometimes I think of God's presence as being a bottomless well. If each person were to come with a cup and dip out of it, they would receive something different. Some would receive the very thing that they were asking for. But others would be surprised by what they would draw out. Instead of finances they might get a cup of faith to trust; or instead of healing they might receive a cup of intimacy and character. Just as the Lord knows every sparrow that falls from the sky, He knows every true need, and thankfully, He always has in abundance what is needed to fulfill it.

Let's Pray:

Dear Lord, you are amazing! I can't even fathom the incredible interweaving in our lives as you minister to individual hearts through a single circumstance. I am thankful that as you feed the birds and clothe the flowers you will also supply all of my needs. You are the well of living water that will never run dry. Thank you for continuously filling my cup according to *Your* riches and glory. In Jesus' Name…Amen!

Reflections:

_____
_____
_____
_____
_____
_____
_____

Friendly Captivity

One night, as my son was channel surfing, a disturbing scene caught my attention. Police investigators were in pursuit of a man who had kidnapped an eight-year-old girl by convincing her he was acting on behalf of her father. When he returned to his residence, the perpetrator introduced the child to a frightened female teen he had abducted eight years earlier. The thought of someone keeping a child prisoner, especially all those years, sent shivers up my spine. Since the house was in a populated neighborhood, I questioned why the now teenaged girl had never stepped outside and called for help when her captor was away—until I realized the restraints that bound her had drawn her into a mental state of "friendly captivity."

When this diabolical man had abducted her as a young girl, he had chained her mind and heart by convincing her he was rescuing her from being arrested, tortured, and taken to a concentration camp. This deception empowered him to win her trust, and to submit to him in a sick, perverted relationship.

In this poor teenager's mind everything was twisted. Evil was good and good was evil. Unfortunately, the ultimate personification of evil, turned out to be the very ones who came to her rescue—the police. Because the teen was firing a weapon at them, the most difficult job of the rescue team was to convince her they were not the enemy. They were finally able to accomplish this by breaking through the lies with seeds of truth.

The first seeds were planted in the form of recollections supplied by her parents, who were brought to the scene. As her father and mother spoke about experiences from her childhood, memories tucked away in the teenager's tormented mind started to surface. Once she began to realize her true identity she released her grip on her weapon—a little. But the real victory didn't come until one of the more obvious deceptions was exposed.

The kidnapper had installed an underground wiring system that would have shocked the teen had she crossed the lawn. When the police announced that the system had been dismantled, the teenage girl did not believe them. But the recently kidnapped eight-year-old did. When the eight-year-old walked outside, the teen went to one of the windows and tore back a corner of the dark paper that was covering the window. She witnessed the eight-year-old run and leap into the arms of one of the officers. Once the lie of imminent death was exposed, other lies soon began to unravel until the teen ultimately decided to take a risk and venture outside.

Although I have never been physically abducted, as I watched the story line unfold, the Lord brought to my remembrance many instances when I had been deceived by others or held captive by lies in my mind. One of the least dramatic occurred in high school during my sophomore year.

My English teacher, Ms. Stewart was a petite, wrinkled 50-something lady with unattractive features, piercing blue eyes, and short-cropped hair. On the first day of class Ms. Stewart became my hero when she held up a large black Bible and announced, "This is the greatest history book ever written!" It wasn't long before I was mesmerized by this unusual woman who lavished approval on me and opened my mind to new ideas while pouring over my poems and essays about searching for reality.

Ms. Stewart was an A+ encourager with an uncanny ability to understand people. She could get even the most disinterested students to "open up." Even though I was a very focused honor student, I was a challenge for Ms. Stewart because I was so timid, as evidenced by my knees knocking together and my brain shutting down anytime I was called upon in class.

From the day she cornered me after class and told me, "You've got a problem," Ms. Stewart began to go to great lengths to help me "come out of my shell." Over a period of time, she won my trust and became my mentor, friend, and confidant. But as she dislodged the questions that troubled my heart and mind, she re-worded them as new information that lined up with her own belief system. Soon the box that she was constantly motivating me to "think outside of," began to contain very little of the Christian ethics with which I had grown up. As a result, not only did I begin to justify sin by spouting that it was judgmental and unloving to call it so, I also began to turn against the very people in my life who were standing for truth. I had fallen into "friendly captivity."

It took quite a few years, but thankfully because of the graciousness of God, I am happy to say there was a day when seeds of truth began to unravel the lies I believed. Lies that up until then, I wasn't even aware were holding me captive. When the darkness was finally peeled away, and the eyes of my heart were opened to see my twisted thinking, my spirit was grieved that, I too, had called evil good and good evil.

Shortly after God began to bring me revelations of His truth, the Lord led me to contact Ms. Stewart and arrange a meeting with her in the teacher's lounge of my old alma mater. As soon as I walked into the room, I announced, "Ms. Stewart, I found reality!"

"What is it?" she answered longingly.

Smiling from ear to ear, I looked into her pleading eyes, and answered, "It's Jesus Christ!" Over the next 20 minutes I shared testimonies of God's healing and deliverance in my life. With tears in her eyes Ms. Stewart asked me to pray for her. I'm sure the angels were rejoicing that day as some of my former teacher's unseen chains crashed to the linoleum. And I celebrated God's goodness, for He had opened the eyes, touched the heart, and brought freedom to yet another captive.

♥ *Heart Encounter* ♥

1. Often times, when I have fallen into *friendly captivity,* I have been unaware that I had even been taken captive. Can you think of a time in your life when you were taken captive without being aware of it? What did it look like?

2. We don't usually just wake up one morning and decide we are going to change our beliefs or compromise our values. As in my experience with Ms. Stewart, like the proverbial frog in the pot that doesn't realize it's being boiled to death until it's too late, it usually happens little by little. There is a familiar saying, *"hind sight is 20/20."* What I was blinded to then is clear as day to me now. When you look back to your times of captivity, can you see the progression of the events that took you there? If so, what were they?

3. I personally believe it is important to both understand

how we fell into captivity and to unveil the lies that kept us there. Why do you think that this would be important?

4. If we know, we won't go. If we truly understand the lies, clearly see the progression, and are fully aware of the consequences, why would we choose to go into captivity? Although there are exceptions, not too many toddlers touch the hot stove twice. After you have been set free, do you desire to go back into bondage?

5. The Bible says in John 8:32 "And you will know the Truth, and the Truth will set you free" (AMP). In his book *Free at Last*, which deals with breaking generational curses, author Larry Huch brings up the point that it is not the truth that sets us free, it is *knowing* the truth that brings us freedom. In light of this statement, how important do you think it is to acquaint yourself with truth through the study of the Word?

6. We can hear truth every day and not receive it. When we study the Word of God, the Holy Spirit illuminates truth to us. Once that truth penetrates our hearts, it becomes our very own. You *know* the truth when you *own* the truth. Can you think of an example when the truth you heard became the truth you owned?

I don't know about you, but anytime I have come to *own truth* I have not been able to keep from sharing, not just my new found freedom, but my new understanding. As the Lord brings us the understanding of the *truth that sets us free*, may we be vessels that take the truth to others. May we also daily "walk it out" so we can show others who are being held captive the way to freedom.

.

Let's Pray:

Father God, Thank you for your incredible love for me. I am so very grateful that you have given me the truth that brings freedom through your Word. Thank you for the times you have brought me deliverance (revealing and breaking off lies and replacing them with truth and demolishing strongholds.) Continue to expose *friendly captivity* in my life. I realize, as in the story of little girl who was kidnapped, that the enemy will often try to deceive me by convincing me that who or what has captured me is right and good. Precious Lord, I pray that you would open my eyes so that I can clearly see evil for what it is. Forgive me for the times when I have either knowing or unknowingly called evil good and good evil. I rejoice, not only in my own deliverance, but also in the realization that you are equipping me to show others the way to freedom. I love you, Lord! You are faithful and good, and your mercy truly endures forever! In Jesus' Name…Amen!

Reflections:

_____

_____

_____

_____

_____

Come Forth!

*A*s I picked up the phone to call my loved one, the words "Come forth!" resonated in my head and heart. In my mind I saw a picture of Lazarus—mummy-like, standing in front of the tomb wrapped in grave clothes of tightly wound linen. "Lord, what are you trying to show me?" I questioned.

I anxiously pushed the numbers on the keypad. I wasn't sure what I should or shouldn't say. "How do I speak the truth in love without coming across as judgmental or preachy?" I thought to myself. "How do I help him realize that God is for him and not against him?"

Although, my loved one had accepted the Lord as a child, years of pain, abuse, and rebellion had pulled him into the world. "God, I'll just have to trust you in this," I murmured. I was then reminded about how the Egyptians amassed treasures and provisions in the tombs. I especially thought about how trinkets were often placed between the linen strips during the mummification process. It was believed that whatever was entombed with the body would provide protection, provision, enjoyment, and wealth in the afterlife, which was nothing more than a futile attempt to satiate future fleshly desires.

I was still picturing a mummy when my dear one answered the phone. His weary voice troubled me. "Lord, give me courage," I prayed. I knew God had heard me because the words began to flow. I told my loved one how Lazarus was still bound when Jesus told him to "come forth." Then after explaining about how the ancient pharaohs amassed wealth for the afterlife, I shared what the Lord had shown me. That all of the things that this loved one had run to for fulfillment were wrapped in the grave clothes that bound him. "The good news," I said, "is that Jesus has spoken, '*Come forth!*'"

I told this young man that I loved him and assured him that I had been daily praying for his emotional healing and deliverance. But since Jesus had already provided the way (after all, He is the Way, the Truth, and the Life), it was his (this young man's) personal choice to take hold of the promises and victories that Christ had already won, and do whatever it would take in order for him to walk out his freedom.

Before we said our good-byes, my dear one shared something he had experienced the night before, which had softened his heart. After listening to him, I reiterated God's unconditional love for him, and assured him that I would continue to pray for him. When I hung up, I not only found myself basking in the peace that passes all understanding, I was once again in awe of how God orchestrates divine appointments in order to lavish His love upon us, His children, even while we are still bound.

♥ *Heart Encounter* ♥

1. The night I talked to my loved one, God broke another box in my life. Instead of addressing the destructive elements that were wrapped in the young man's grave clothes (and believe me, I could have pulled out a long list,) I was only led to encourage him that Jesus had already provided the way for his freedom. Do you believe that Jesus has already provided the way for your freedom and for the freedom of your loved ones? Explain.

2. Let's look for a moment at the resurrection of Lazarus in John 11. By the time Jesus arrived at the tomb, Lazarus had been dead four days. In John 11:39, Martha even exclaimed, "But Lord, by this time he [is decaying and] throws off an offensive odor!" (AMP). Wow! That would be an understatement! Everyone around, except Jesus, was well aware that Lazarus was *too far gone*; there could be no help for him now! Have you ever felt that you had gone too far in your

sin for the Lord to bring life back to you? Or perhaps, you have loved ones who *stinketh* as they are decaying in their grave clothes. What do you think Jesus would say?

3. Notice that Jesus didn't carry Lazarus out of the tomb; nor did He have him unwrapped before He called him out. He simply called him forth. Many times, when you and I are in our own muck and mire with the stench of death on us we expect someone to rescue us. Have you ever felt stuck because no one has come to carry you out of your grave? Explain.

4. Or maybe, conversely, you have been the one who keeps trying to carry out the corpses. Are you trying to remove the grave clothes from smelly, dead bodies while they are still entombed?

5. Jesus summoned, and Lazarus walked out. Although Jesus declares life over us and our loved ones, it has to be walked out. I think about how difficult it must have been for Lazarus to walk. Since he was bound in his grave attire, his feet were probably pretty well tied together, causing him to take tiny awkward steps to get to the entrance of the tomb. Often times, when Jesus has called me out of the tombs in my life, I have

found myself taking tiny awkward steps on my road to freedom. How about you? Is there an area that you are bound in now? If so, what is it?

6. The most important thing is not *how* we walk; it is *that* we walk. Before the grave clothes can be removed, you and I have to choose to walk out of the tomb. No one can make that choice for us; nor can we make that choice for someone else. Since Jesus has already provided the way to freedom, we just have to make an agreement with what He has already done and *come forth*! Have you made that choice?

7. When we are bound we often want instant results; however, we need to realize that we didn't get that way over night. It might take some time, and the love of brothers and sisters in Christ, to help unwind the lies that got us where we are. Are you willing to trust the process and the people God places in your life on your way to freedom?

Are you bound? Have you wrapped yourself in the lies of this world as you have tried to find fulfillment in what does not satisfy? Jesus has spoken, "I am the way, the truth, and the life. No one comes to the Father except through me" (John 14:6). Do you want truth? Do you want life? Do you want freedom? Then receive the command of Jesus and "come forth." Come as you are. Come anyway you have to—taking awkward little baby steps, if need be. Just come!

Let's Pray:

Lord, thank you for being the *way maker.* You have already provided *the way* for my freedom, my healing, my deliverance, and my destiny. All I have to do is to receive the life you have given me and *walk it out.* Loose me from the desires for the things of this world that have been tied up in my binding. I want to live for you. Thank you for loving me. Give me courage, patience, and wisdom, and bring people into my life to help me walk in the freedom you have given me. In Jesus Name…Amen!

Reflections:

_____
_____
_____
_____
_____
_____
_____
_____
_____

The Hummingbird

One morning, while walking through her back yard, an old woman *almost* stepped on a small object that was lying on the ground. When she bent down to get a closer look, she realized it was a hummingbird. The small creature couldn't move because it was tangled in a fine strand of thread. "Oh! You poor little thing," the woman voiced as she cautiously scooped up the hummingbird into her hands. The frightened little bird immediately began to flutter. The old woman slowly spread her fingers apart and locked her thumbs together to form a cage so as not to damage the bird's shimmery fragile wings. As the old woman peeked through her fingers, compassion continued to stir in her heart. The tiny bird's delicate beauty delighted her as much as its unlikely predicament astounded her. "How on earth did this little creature get so bound?" she thought to herself.

Taking slow, deliberate steps, the old woman crossed her yard and entered her house. As she placed the tiny captive in a small, shallow box on her kitchen table, she once again looked down in amazement at the thread wrapped around the bird's delicate feet. "It's Okay, little one," she cooed. "I'm going to help you. You will soon be free."

The old woman went into the other room and returned with a pair of manicure scissors. Then she set to work, softy humming a joyful tune. As she ever-so-gently held the fluttering hummingbird with one hand, she meticulously separated and snipped the strands of thread. If she cut through all of the wrapped thread at once, she was sure to wound the tiny creature. "Oh, Lord, help me," she whispered. As she worked to free the hummingbird's tiny bound feet, the Lord reminded her of the story about Lazarus in the 11th chapter of John, pointing out that just as the hummingbird needed her help, Lazarus needed his friends to help remove his grave clothes.

When the final thread was unwound, the old woman took the bird back outside and set it back in its nest, right where it belonged. It was now free—free to rest, free to fly—free to do whatever it had been created to do.

♥ *Heart Encounter* ♥

1. John 11:44 tells us that Lazarus was bound hand and foot when he exited the tomb. Jesus instructed the

people to "Free him of the burial wrappings and let him go" (AMP). Most likely, the people assisting Lazarus did not approach him with a large pair of scissors or knives, making a few strategic and possibly harmful cuts. Instead, just like the woman removing the thread from the hummingbird, they had to be gentle as they unwrapped his grave clothes. How do you believe this applies to the role of the body of Christ today?

2. When the old woman first picked up the hummingbird, she made a cage for it with her hands. Once inside the house, she opened her hands and placed the bird in a box. She only tightly held onto the bird when it was time to remove the string. How could the boundaries the woman provided for the bird correlate to the boundaries we need to set in place when helping others "get free"?

3. As we help others gain freedom from their bondages, we can sometimes get overly caught up in attempting to remove the objects that bind the person (drugs, sex, alcohol, pornography, etc.) without bringing life and truth to the inner man. Why is it important to understand that physical bondages are the outward manifestations of deeper heart problems?

4. Once the hummingbird was loosed, it was free to function according to its design. How could this apply to our desire to see others released of their bondages?

5. Just as the old woman asked God for help as she was unbinding the hummingbird, we need to seek God on behalf of others. When helping people gain freedom, it's easy for you and me to get frustrated and expect too much too soon. True change begins in the heart. God could be moving mightily and changing a person's heart, long before we may see the evidence of change. That is why it is crucial to pray for wisdom and understanding. How can the wisdom of Psalms 85:10 equip us to reach out to those in bondage?

6. The union of mercy, loving-kindness, and truth equate to powerful, anointed ministry. Although we do have to put forth the effort and speak truth in order to unwind the grave clothes, we also have to be cautious not to be so harsh as to wound the person. Do you reach out to others with mercy, love and truth? Explain.

Just as the old woman used her manicure scissors to cut the thread, God equips us with tools we can utilize to remove grave clothes. Although love, truth, wisdom, and coming into agreement with God's Word are powerful tools, I have discovered that prayer is the most effective tool we have been given. I actually think of it as being more of a weapon than a tool.

During a season when I was reaching out to some wounded women, the Lord told me, *"If you want to help people get free, you have to do the hard work of prayer."* As I began to pray for extended periods of time, I saw lives change. I ended up getting so excited about what God was doing, that after awhile praying for hours no longer seemed hard. It was exhilarating. Do you want to see lives change? Then pray. Pray! PRAY! **PRAY!** Not only does prayer equip us with grace, wisdom, mercy, and strength; it also causes battles to be won in the heavens as well as releasing divine opportunities on earth.

Lets Pray:

Dear Lord, continue to show me the areas of my life where I need freedom, and equip me to bring truth to others. Help me to keep in mind that lies and hurts keep people bound, not just the vices that have become intertwined in their grave clothes. Give me wisdom and teach me healthy boundaries. Let me walk in your love, mercy, and truth as I pray for and minister to those who are in captivity. In Jesus' Name…Amen!

Reflections:

_____
_____
_____
_____
_____
_____
_____
_____
_____

Perfect Peace

Sometimes, God calls us to step out of our comfort zone and walk with someone for a season. Then He closes the door. But what happens when you and I try to take people beyond where we are supposed to take them? And how do we know when and where to draw the line?

When my oldest son was a baby, I began selling Avon door-to-door to help make ends meet. As I was out and about, I met many interesting and sometimes difficult people, but an old double amputee named Charlie had to be my biggest challenge. The afternoon I knocked on Charlie's door and introduced myself as an Avon representative, he growled, "Does it look like I can use AVON?!" and slammed the door in my face. As I was briskly walking away, the Lord told me, *"Go back and ask him if you can help him with anything."*

I'll skip mentioning my first, second, or even third responses. But I *will* tell you that after I climbed upon the altar and let God kill about 105 pounds of ugly flesh, I returned to his door with a big smile on my face and offered my assistance.

I was really hoping Charlie would growl, "No, go away!" and slam the door again. Well, he didn't. Charlie not only welcomed me into his apartment, he immediately began to comprise a shopping list and point to his urine saturated laundry. *Yeah!* Hence began my year-long lesson in humility as I took Charlie on weekly errands and helped him with his household chores.

However, the most difficult thing for me was not serving Charlie—it was listening to him. Charlie was an angry, bitter World War II vet who was furious with God, disconnected from his family, and still hated his deceased ex-wife, who he affectionately referred to as "Satan's wife." He was also extremely prejudiced because it was easier for him to proclaim racism than deal with the guilt of having followed orders to shoot deserters in his unit. While recounting his "war experiences," Charlie's contorted face would mirror his contorted soul. He would clamp his hands around his wheelchair arms and spew out obscenities against the soldiers who had fled, and against God for never caring about anyone—ever!

No matter the day or the circumstances, Charlie could find plenty of negative things to say. So I was a bit surprised when he agreed to let me pray for him when he was diagnosed with cancer. "They are going to cut me open next week," He informed me. "You can pray, but it probably won't do any good."

I immediately went home and called some ministry

prayer chains to pray for Charlie's healing. The next week when Charlie told me that the doctor had found nothing when they cut him open, I literally leapt in the air saying, "Praise God! He healed YOU!" After grumbling something about he didn't understand why I was so excited and it being just a coincidence, there was never any mention of cancer or healing again.

As the year drew to a close, another pregnancy and a move across town forced me to turn Charlie's care over to another. I didn't hear from him again until after our daughter was born. That is why I was both surprised and alarmed the afternoon he called and begged me to come over. His voice was shaky as he said, "I need you to come right away. It's an emergency!" When I asked him what the emergency was about, he insisted, "I can't tell you over the phone."

Since he wouldn't give me any information and remained adamant about me coming, I didn't hesitate to ask my husband Joe, who had once visited Charlie with me, to watch our "little ones." I grabbed the keys and headed out the door. When I started the car, I heard in my spirit: *"If you go alone you are not coming back!"* I thought to myself, "That's weird!" and then proceeded to shift in reverse. I heard yet again: *"If you go alone you are not coming back!"* In my mind I saw a picture of Charlie shooting me.

After hesitating a minute longer, I told God, "Well, maybe it's my time to die," to which He assured me it was not and told me to go ask Joe to come with me. I removed the keys and went back into the apartment. A bit confused and frustrated, I told Joe both what God had told me, and what I had seen. To my astonishment, he agreed to go with me.

During the ride over, I had a strange sense of peace and envisioned angels surrounding us. When we parked the car, the Lord very emphatically told me that I was to let Joe go first and follow a ways behind with the kids. When Charlie opened the door and saw Joe, not only was he shocked, he began stammering: "Uh… Joe…I didn't…expect to see *you*!" Then he looked down at the gun in his hand and said, "Joe, do you want to see my gun?" Joe took the gun, opened it, and replied, "Nice gun, Charlie—and it's loaded." I thought to myself, "Oh my Gosh! He *was* going to kill me!"

As we visited with Charlie that afternoon, my peace never left me, even when he was lashing out at me for believing in God and barking that his deceased ex-wife had been talking to him in his dreams. That afternoon before we left, I asked Charlie what the emergency was. "Emergency?" he replied.

"Yes, the emergency you called me about."

"Oh,…that." He hemmed and hawed a bit, then pulled his checkbook from the drawer. "I…uh...I need you to balance my checkbook for me. I just can't get it to balance." I took a look at his perfectly balanced checkbook, told him it was already balanced, returned it to him and left—still keeping my peace, but certain that, for me, the door to Charlie's was permanently closed.

I have no doubt that God originally told me to help Charlie. I also have no regrets. I have never been angry with Charlie or God about the way our relationship ended. (I later heard through someone else that he had become more receptive to the Lord.) All of these things transpired when I was in a season where I was living in incredible fear, so I was amazed that I experienced absolutely *no fear* that afternoon, even when I realized how much Charlie hated me—or Christ in me. And I am, still to this day, in awe—not just because of God's protection in the matter, but also for His *perfect peace* in the midst of it.

♥ *Heart Encounter* ♥

1. Ephesians 6:10-20 talks about putting on the armor of God. In order to stand against the wiles of the devil, you and I not only need to recognize that we "wrestle not against flesh and blood," but that we need to be correctly outfitted. Just as a soldier would not go into battle wearing a bathing suit and flip flops, you and I should not battle without *suiting up*. Right along with listing the helmet, the breastplate, the sword, the shield, and the belt, the Apostle Paul includes the shoes of peace. What do you think would be the significance of wearing *these* shoes?

2. "Peace I leave with you, My peace I give to you; not as the world gives do I give to you. Let not your heart be troubled, neither let it be afraid" (John 14:27). Although God does not give us a "spirit of fear," a *troubled heart* can be an indication that something is *not right*. When our hearts are *troubled* you and I need to pay attention and ask God for understanding. When our *peace* returns we can go forward or be redirected according to His wisdom. The day Charlie called I didn't have peace until Joe went with me. But I had tremendous peace when I followed the Lord's direction. Have you ever stepped forward without peace and later regretted it? Explain.

3. There was an occasion a few years later when I ignored both my *troubled spirit* and the Lord's warning. The trauma that resulted had huge consequences that are still playing out today. Although I have seen the Lord restore many broken pieces I still have regrets in moving forward without peace. Can you relate? Explain?

4. Often, you and I will get redirected by the Holy Spirit as we are "on the way" in serving the Lord. An example of this would be the Macedonian call in Acts 16:6-10. When the scripture says "They were forbidden by the Holy Spirit" to preach the word in

Asia and Bithynia, I wonder if they stopped to listen because of an absence of peace. God ended up giving Paul a vision that redirected him and his companions to Macedonia. I was given a vision and a warning that redirected me when I was "on the way" to help Charlie. Have you ever been redirected when you were "on the way?"

5. Being redirected isn't always about danger. I can think of many incidents where I was redirected because my *spirit was troubled* that ended in incredible blessings of either divine appointments or divine opportunities. Jesus listened to His father and went where the Father sent Him. Don't you think we should do likewise?

You and I need to be careful to listen to the Lord and stay in the place of peace every step of the way—especially when we are reaching out to hurting people. As I had been warned by an ex-cop in another situation years later, "Nice people sometimes get killed!" God might tell you to give to or feed a homeless man, but He doesn't *usually* tell you to take him home. He might tell you to pray for and encourage someone in sin, but not to invite them into your family, especially if they are battling lust and you have children. If your spirit is *troubled* concerning a person or a situation, stop and pray and re-establish the parameters. While perfect love, the love of Jesus casts out all fear, *perfect peace* (Jesus Himself) will guide you. Isaiah 26:3 "You will keep *him* in perfect peace, *Whose* mind *is* stayed *on You*, Because he trusts in You."

Let's Pray:

Father God, thank you for leading and guiding me. When I lose my peace, help me to stop and ask you for wisdom. You not only lead me in the way of peace, but you *are* my peace. Thank you for allowing my spirit to be *troubled* when I am stepping out of your will, and for giving me the *peace that passes understanding* when I am where I should be. Thank you, Father, for your Son— my Lord and Savior—the *Prince of Peace.* In Jesus' Name...Amen!

Reflections:

_____

_____

_____

_____

_____

_____

_____

_____

Humane?

The monstrous machinery beckoned the wide-eyed wonder of our children as the ground was being cleared for the new houses that were going up around us. Invariably, every morning at the crack of dawn, our entire household would awaken to the familiar rumble of bulldozers and the whining of hydraulics which seem to say, "Come and see! Come and see!" Like clockwork, our children would quickly dress and scurry outside to observe the above ground activity. However, as our attention was riveted to the construction sites above the ground, we remained oblivious to the scurrying taking place underground—that is, at first, anyway.

We were soon to discover as the ground was being disturbed, that there was an influx of little critters who decided that they needed to find new residences, and lucky for us, the majority of them chose ours. Consequently, in a short while, our home was literally crawling with roaches, scorpions, and other assorted insects and arachnids.

Being the kind hosts that we were, we bought and administered sprays and laid out little delicacies in the form of baits. We even were so hospitable as to pay for tiny hotels in which our unwanted guests could retire (permanently). Although these courtesies pretty much eliminated the bug problem, when Simon Squeaker III and his entire family (extended relatives included) decided to move in, we were at a loss.

I'll never forget the day I first met Simon. I was in the kitchen minding my own business when something scurried past my feet. I bolted up on top of the counter while discovering that I could hit a new high octave. My newly acquired vocal skill alerted my husband Joe, who came running into the kitchen. Soon it was unanimously decided that the Squeakers would be vacating our residence in the near future. The only question was their mode of departure.

As a little girl I remember crying when my father held up a trap revealing a tiny mouse with a broken neck. I didn't want to expose my kids to that, and poisons weren't an option since we had small children. So how do you get rid of mice otherwise? Fortunately, the solution seemed to come quickly as I was talking to my neighbor the next morning. "You don't really want to *kill* them do you?" she admonished." Why don't you get a humane trap?"

Humane trap? Hmmm. I had never heard of such a thing, but I liked the way it sounded. So early the next morning, I ventured off to the store and purchased a genuine humane mouse trap. Basically, a humane mouse trap is nothing more than a small, hard plastic, see-through box with a swinging door. You place the bait, peanut butter, cheese, or whatever inside and invite the mouse for dinner. The mouse runs in, bites the entrée and the door swings shut trapping him inside, right? WRONG! We were getting ready to discover why the trap was called humane!

Simon and the rest of his family seemed to really enjoy their late night snacks and quickly perfected the art of dine and dash. Actually, since they were being fed so well, I imagined the day would come when they would no longer fit in the trap due to obesity. Apparently, the Squeakers were also health conscious since they would keep us up half the night doing little mice gymnastics throughout the house in order to stay in shape. Before long, instead of anticipating rodent funerals, we were beginning to wonder if the Squeaker family would set some kind of record in mice longevity.

However, the day finally arrived when one of the Squeakers didn't fare so well, and we finally had us a mouse. Actually inside the box it looked more like a mouse in a house. When my husband showcased the small trophy to the children and me, we wondered, "Okay, now what are we supposed to do with it?"

It was decided that if we released the mouse back into its natural habitat it would just come back for dessert, so the only solution would be to dispose of it. Now you have to remember—the whole idea was to be *humane.* So the question we had to ask ourselves was "How do you humanely execute a mouse?" Of course the way the pathetic creature was looking at us, seemingly begging for mercy, didn't help much. After a short consultation, Joe decided to flush it down the toilet. As the curious little procession surrounded the porcelain bowl, the mouse was tossed into the swirling waters below. Unfortunately, we didn't count on our Squeaker member being an Olympic swimmer. Pathetically, the more the toilet was flushed; the faster the terrified rodent frantically paddled his little feet in an attempt to climb the side of the bowl in order to avoid the "whirlpool of death."

After a few failed attempts at flushing him, my husband instructed one of the children to bring him a plastic cup. Upon delivery, he slammed it down and crushed the mouse's skull. As he proceeded to flush our little captive down into his watery grave, the children's horrified faces said enough. This mode of demise definitely did *not* register very high on the humane scale!

After witnessing the horror that had just taken place in the bathroom, I drove to the store and bought a few packages of those good old-fashioned spring loaded traps. For weeks afterward, I would jerk awake to a snapping sound in the middle of the night, but I could easily go back to sleep since I knew that although another Squeaker family member had met its demise—it had happened humanely!

The other night the Lord brought back to my remembrance the above incident. As I began to write, I thought about how when you and I are wrestling with difficult choices we often opt for the seemingly least painful route. Let's face it. Some decisions are just plain going to hurt. Putting them off or feeding them by candy coating them only extends the inevitable. I have learned the hard way, from more experiences than I care to mention, that although it might not always seem like it, sometimes the most humane way to handle a difficult situation is just to act quickly and break its neck.

♥ *Heart Encounter* ♥

1. I can think of numerous times in my life when instead of making a necessary "tough love" kind of decision, I ended up feeding the very problem I was trying to eliminate. Can you think of a time when this was the case?

2. The Bible tells us in Ephesians 4:25, "Therefore, rejecting all falsity *and* being done now with it, let everyone express the truth with his neighbor, for we are all parts of one body *and* members of one another" (AMP). Speaking the truth in love might at times offend, but it attacks the problem directly and breaks

the neck of the enemy. Can you give an example when you have seen truth in love bring life to a situation? Can you think of situations where feeding a lie, even out of good intentions, made the problem worse? What were the results?

3. James 1:22 says, "But be doers of the Word [obey the message], and not merely listeners to it, betraying yourselves [into deception by reasoning contrary to the Truth]" (AMP). There will be times when all of our *good intentions* will be in vain. Some situations require decisive and abrupt action. Let's face it, there are some patterns that need to be broken, some friendships that need to be severed, and some lies that need to be crushed. In these situations what could be the result of trying to figure out a seemingly "more humane" way, thus, putting off the inevitable?

Looking back, I have many regrets because of decisions I made in order not to offend people. Unfortunately, I am still continuing to live with some of the consequences today. When the Lord says sever—we need to sever, no matter what or who it involves. Before a friend gave me the book *Boundaries* I repeatedly enabled some of the people I was trying to help. I was so concerned about hurting their feelings that I didn't practice *tough love*. What should have been a quick death would become a long drawn out process in which the very problems that needed to be eliminated were fed. The slow, agonizing progression that inevitably resulted, cost more time, money, and consequences than it should have. I would encourage you to ask the Lord if there is something that needs to be severed in your life. If He reveals something to you, then pray for courage and do the most humane thing—act quickly and break its neck.

Let's Pray:

Dear Lord, forgive me for all of the times when I have fed situations that I should have just severed. Teach me truth and help me to put into action what I learn. Help me to trust you and give me courage to obey you, no matter how difficult it may seem. I know that you love me. I chose to place my trust in you. In Jesus' Name…Amen!

Reflections:

_____

_____

_____

_____

_____

_____

_____

_____

Breaking the Power

At what point do you and I open the doors that lead to moral failure? Is it with the first thought, glance, or action? Or is it when we—like Eve, when confronted with the forbidden—become convinced that God is unjustly keeping us from something we need or desire? "After all," we rationalize, "if God is good, wouldn't our happiness be of supreme importance to Him?" One thing is for certain, whether they are opened out of vulnerability or justification, the doors lead to a stage where as in the lyrics of the Casting Crowns song *Slow Fade* "black and white soon turn to gray." And we find ourselves starring in a drama for which we never auditioned.

Shortly after the birth of our fourth child, a man named Tom moved into the apartment next door with his two young sons. Our oldest son Joshua soon became fast friends with his oldest son Tyler. Since Tyler was spending so much time at our house, it wasn't long before Tom began to stop by our place on a regular basis "just to chat".

I really couldn't explain why, but I felt uncomfortable with Tom's initial visits. Since my husband Joe didn't seem to mind the impromptu house calls or the compliments Tom would intermittently throw my way, I ignored my gut feelings and rationalized that maybe God had brought Tom into our lives for a purpose. So I took advantage of the opportunity at hand, and began to witness to him. But opportunity soon turned to oppression the morning Tom showed up in Joe's absence *just* to tell me what a great mom I was.

Since I was in a difficult marriage, I knew I was vulnerable. I thought I could protect myself if I set up some simple safeguards, such as making sure that the children were around during Tom's visits. I also tried to stop his flattery by changing the conversation whenever he complimented me. But Tom was persistent. The compliments kept coming.

During one of his visits, Tom told me, "I can't believe how bad Joe treats you!" and then followed up with all of the wonderful things *he* would do for me if he were married to me. From that point on, I knew I was in trouble. As my guard began to come down, my attention-starved heart lapped up his words like a thirsty fawn—words that not only swaddled me in false security, but also painted a picture of luscious green pastures.

I felt like a neglected, starved sheep staring longingly through the fence at the rich grass I could never have.

The more I stared, the more I desired to be free. Although I began to rationalize my ever growing feelings for Tom, even my rationalizations couldn't excuse what I knew was wrong. Eventually, I cried out to God: "Lord, You have to take these feelings away!"

Ironically, the more I prayed against Tom's image in my head and heart, the more the battle escalated. Before I realized what was happening I was engulfed in a dense, dark fog of which I saw no way out. In order to relieve the guilt I was feeling, I decided to go to my husband for help. I thought his disapproval of Tom, or better yet, his approval of me, would put an end to my temptation. So one night in a manipulative, weak attempt to come clean and draw in reinforcements, I flippantly commented to Joe, "It's pretty bad when the neighbor compliments your wife and you don't." Wow! Was that the wrong thing to say! The smart aleck comment Joe made as he laughed and walked away left me feeling humiliated and defenseless. It was obvious that the outcome of this battle would result in my either staying in the life I hated or jumping the fence to the life I thought I wanted. "Our marriage was a disaster from the beginning," I rationalized, "It's doomed to fail anyway, so why hang on any longer?"

I wanted to serve God, even sacrificially, but the taste of possible love and acceptance was hard to resist. The resulting guilt and shame that held me captive made it difficult to picture an alternative, much less see myself as a victor. Any time I thought about confiding in someone or asking for prayer, I dismissed the idea because I was afraid people would think that I was a horrible person. But I eventually became so tormented and overrun by passion, I knew I had to change my position, humble myself, face my fears, and ask for help.

My help came in the form of my pastor's wife and a dear friend. Instead of the condemnation I expected, they showered me with compassion and concern. As I confessed the sins of my mind and heart, they prayed for me. In the midst of their unconditional love and support, I was instantly set free. When they broke off the deception and severed the plans of the enemy, all of the intense emotions I had toward Tom immediately ceased.

A few weeks later, a young woman moved in with Tom, and the way he *really treated* his women surfaced. As the quiet residence next door turned into an abusive, alcoholic war zone, I daily became more thankful for God's intervention. But my thankfulness reached new heights the afternoon a blue-eyed, thirty-something woman came to my door looking for Tom. Apparently, our "friend" Tom was a clever artist, for he had been painting a picture of luscious green pastures for her at the same time he had for me. The only difference was she had left her husband to claim her painting.

My heart went out to the woman as I directed her to Tom's apartment, where his new girlfriend greeted her. Although I couldn't even imagine the confusion and heartache she must have felt, as I watched the woman slowly drive away while trying to see through her tears.

The stark reality hit me that I could easily have been in her place.

A married friend once confided about a similar struggle she had, but unfortunately she was paying the consequences of jumping the fence. She said she thought about calling when she was in the midst of her battle, but she was too ashamed, so she confessed her struggle to no one. The result was an affair. After consoling and counseling a bit, I told her about Tom and explained how the power of confession exposed and annihilated the plans of the enemy when I was tempted. I then encouraged her to always call when she was tempted.

Unfortunately, when I was ministering to singles I saw this over and over again. Way too often the calls came after the falls. That is why it is so very important, whether you and I are married or single, to seek out godly accountability with people in whom we can confide, and who will pray for us when we are struggling with temptation or sin.

I can honestly say regarding not only the temptation towards Tom, but also in other incidents in my life, that I have seen the power of sin broken over and over again as I have confessed my sinful thoughts and received prayer. But that was not always the case. For many years, my pride kept me from both confessing and coming before the altar because I cared more about my reputation then reconciliation. But thank God, I now realize that sin is sin, and it doesn't matter what anyone thinks. I want freedom! Repentance cleanses, but confession breaks the yolk.

♥ *Heart Encounter* ♥

1. Can you think of a time when you didn't confess your struggle when tempted? What was the result?

2. In contrast, can you think of a time when you did confess the battle that was before you? What was the result of bringing your struggle into the light?

3. There is a reason why James 5:16 instructs us to "Confess to one another therefore your faults (your slips, your false steps, your offenses, your sins) and pray [also] for one another, that you may be healed *and* restored [to a spiritual tone of mind and heart]" (AMP). Do you think God knew that you and I would be tempted?

4. God loves us so much that He has already set in His Word the ways for us to be victorious. I find in my own life that shame is the number one way the enemy keeps my mouth shut when I am in the midst of a battle. If the devil can keep me more focused on what

others think than on doing whatever it takes to over come, he can keep me bound. Have you ever found yourself wanting freedom, but too ashamed to share your battle with others? Give an example.

5. Guilt can lead us to repentance because it tells us that we have done something wrong. But shame brings condemnation because it tells us that something is wrong with us. What does the Word of God tell us about condemnation in Romans 8:1?

6. If the Word tells us that "there is no condemnation for those who are in Christ Jesus" then who is it that condemns us?

7. In Revelation 12:9-10, we are told that the devil is the accuser of the brethren. Should we listen to him? The Bible tells us that there will be a day when the devil is cast out completely, but until that day, we can learn to cast him out daily, sometimes even minute by minute. How can we do this?

8. 2 Corinthians 10:5 tells us: "[Inasmuch as we] refute arguments *and* theories *and* reasonings and every proud *and* lofty thing that sets itself up against the

[true] knowledge of God; and we lead every thought *and* purpose away captive into the obedience of Christ (the Messiah, the anointed One)" (AMP). Simply put, we need to take the thoughts of condemnation captive and replace them with what Jesus would say. What does Jesus say?

I personally am afraid to think where I could have gone—not just in my mind, but in my actions—had the Lord not helped me to risk what others thought and confess my sin struggle. As you and I take the thoughts of shame and condemnation captive, we can be assured that we are not alone. God loves us and wants us to be victorious. If you're currently struggling, I would encourage you to ask Him for wisdom. As you place your trust in Him, He will show you a safe place where you can be counseled in what you *need* to hear (not necessarily in what you *want* to hear) in order to bring you freedom.

Let's Pray:

Dear Lord, thank you for forgiving me of my sins. Thank you also for showing me how to break the power of sin by confessing and praying with others. (James 5:16.) Give me wisdom as to whom I can confide in, and break off pride and help me share what has tormented me and held me captive. Help me realize that it is your perfect love that not only casts out fear, but also desires for me to be free. Open my eyes to see what I need to see, open my ears so I can hear what I need to hear, and open my heart so I can receive your truth. Saturate me in healing prayer that breaks the power and brings forth the victory. I love you, Lord! In Jesus' Name...Amen!

Reflections:

_____

_____

_____

_____

_____

_____

_____

_____

Disappointment?

*A*lthough I enjoy Christian retreats, usually by the afternoon of the second day, unless I'm taking notes, my mind starts wandering. I'm not sure whether I forgot my pen, or if I just decided to "enjoy the ride" as my thoughts wove between the lanes of the present and the future during a retreat in Tucson a few years back. But I'll never forget how quickly I suddenly slammed on the brakes and sat to full attention when the speaker mentioned the word *disappointment.*

Disappointment—*Disappointment*—**Disappointment!** As the word resounded in my head, an onslaught of images flashed before me like a myriad of haunting phantoms. However, as quickly as the ghosts had come, they vanished when the Lord broke through the torment and confusion and spoke to my heart: *"I will turn all of your disappointments into appointments!"*

As the unexpected words of my Loving Father stirred my spirit, I began to explore the immensity of their potential. Not *one* of my disappointments...not *two*...or...*three*...or *four*...but *all* of them! Every single disappointment in my life was going to be turned into a divine appointment by my Heavenly Father! What a miracle! What an incredible promise! I devoured the seed of hope like a choice morsel.

During the days that followed I ruminated on the ingested seed, until one morning the bud of understanding burst forth. Revelation after revelation began to unveil themselves. Not only had the Lord already given me many divine appointments with others in sharing the testimonies He had brought forth out of the disappointments in my life, He had also orchestrated many divine appointments with *me* as He had met me in my darkest hours.

So many times, when we are sinking in the porta-potties of our lives, the Lord reaches down in the midst of our circumstances and ushers us into His very throne room. The places of our greatest woundings become the operating rooms of our souls where the boundaries of our hearts are enlarged and even the most diabolical attacks of the enemy can open doors to intimacy with God. Disappointments are turned into divine appointments as the clay meets the Potter, the afflicted meets the Healer, the captive meets the Deliver, and the abused meets the Restorer.

During those painful moments where disillusionment clouds our understanding, the lightning of heavenly revelation strikes through the storm and pierces our souls.

Encouragement then replaces discouragement, and we discover new courage as our prisons birth the passions that propel us into our purpose.

In the midst of our disappointments, good seed is sown in fertile soil, yielding a double portion. Once the seed of revelation is sown, it will in time, under the Master's care, produce testimony that is shared out of a thankful heart—testimony that sows more life-giving seed. Hence, the hour of disappointment having met with the divine is transformed and now awaits divine opportunity.

In sharing how the Lord helped us forgive, you and I can minister forgiveness to others. In being healed and delivered, you and I can become vessels of healing and deliverance. The grace, encouragement, and comfort that has been extended *to* us is now extended *through* us.

Romans 8:28 promises us that whatever the enemy had intended for evil, God will turn for good. You and I *will* see this promise fulfilled when disappointments are turned into appointments. But, thankfully, since God is into multiplication, He will turn it for good, not just once, but over and over and over again.

♥ *Heart Encounter* ♥

1. Unmet expectations often bring disappointment. What are some disappointments you have experienced?

2. Did God meet you in the midst of your dark hours? If so, how?

3. As believers, you and I have opportunities for greater intimacy with the Lord in the difficult times. However, I believe that if we look back, we can see how the Lord met us when we weren't even aware of His love or His presence. Can you remember some of those times? If so, what were they?

4. What do these "meetings" tell you about God's unfailing love for you? Years ago, the Lord ministered to me through a song by David Meece called *His Love is Reaching*. It's about how God's love was reaching out and pulling us through difficulties without us realizing it. Ask the Holy Spirit to bring you revelation of times when His love was reaching out to you and touching your life when you may not have been aware of it. What is He revealing to you?

5. Read 2 Corinthians 1:3-4. Verse 3 identifies God as being the Father of sympathy and the God of all comfort. In the beginning of verse 4 we are reminded that He "…comforts (consoles and encourages) us in every trouble (calamity and affliction)" (AMP). Isn't

that incredible? His comfort is always there; we just have to receive it.

6. Now read the rest of verse 4: "...so that we may also be able to comfort (console and encourage those who are in any kind of trouble *or* distress, with the comfort (consolation and encouragement) with which we ourselves are comforted (consoled and encouraged) by God" (AMP). I love this part! That's the double portion! Having met with the divine, you and I are now able to be used divinely. How can this scripture bring you hope when you are facing disappointments?

The scriptures are full of divine appointments (encounters with the Lord.). As we study the lives of such people as Jacob, David, Job, Hannah, Paul, and Silas—just to name a few—we can definitely see how the Lord powerfully met people in the midst of their darkest hours. He also continues to meet people today through the written testimonies of their lives.

It is reassuring to me to know that not only does God desire to draw us close and bring us comfort, He also desires us to be His vessels to bring comfort to others. How precious it is to trust in Him, knowing that He will bring forth good and give us *beauty for ashes!*

Let's Pray:

Precious Lord, I am in awe when I think of your love for me! You never leave me nor forsake me. You faithfully draw close to me, bringing me encouragement and comfort during the difficult times. Thank you for meeting me in the midst of my disappointments and turning for good everything that the enemy has intended for evil. Continue to bring forth the double portion as you sow fertile seed in my heart and open the doors for opportunities for me to share your love and truth with others. In Jesus Name…Amen!

Reflections:

_____
_____
_____
_____
_____
_____
_____
_____
_____

Releasing the Debt

While I was getting ready to go to work one morning in 2010, God spoke to my spirit: "Invest in your grandchildren. When Beckie and her husband move to their next duty station, you are to go with them."

I wish I could say I was excited, but I felt quite the opposite. Although I absolutely adore my kids and grandkids, I was praying for a husband, not a household. My dreams of Cinderella and Prince Charming immediately morphed into Andy Griffith and Aunt Bee. "This is not the storybook ending I'd been praying for!" I whined.

Over the next few days, as I prayed about leaving my job of six years and stepping into another "faith season," I thought about everything that would have to fall into place in order for the move to happen. God would have to bring my daughter and son-in-law into agreement and give us favor with their new military base. I would also need to downsize and rent a storage unit for a year. All I really "knew" was that I was supposed to move to somewhere at sometime. The whole idea seemed ridiculous!

In my heart I knew this move was about more than just family because God was also burdening my heart to minister to military wives. So after praying a bit more, I called my daughter Beckie and presented the idea to her. Having a very active 18 month-old who had already discovered how to light the toaster on fire, flood the kitchen, and throw absolutely everything into the trashcan, and another little one on the way—she was, of course, elated. A month later I took a mini-vacation to visit Rebekah and her family, and after the three of us had discussed the pros and cons, we decided to move forward.

I have learned that when God begins something, He brings it to completion, and that is exactly what He did. The duty station ended up being in Maryland. The timing ended up being March, and the means ended up being many instances of supernatural provision, which would all follow on the heels of a test and an incredible unexpected blessing.

One morning, while I was packing up boxes to put into storage, I grabbed a book off of the shelf I did not recognize. After quickly reading a few testimonies about God miraculously meeting people when they took steps of faith in their finances, I decided it was a keeper and tossed it in a box. When I turned around to grab the next stack of books I heard in my spirit: "Call everyone who owes you money and release their debts."

Ouch! Between family members who owed me back rent and repayment of loans, and a friend who hadn't finished paying for the van I sold to her, we were talking about almost $6,000. That was six-grand I was hoping would be my solution for income the following year—so much for security!

Since I was outgrowing my temper tantrum stage, instead of arguing with God, I reluctantly but obediently picked up the phone and called the first person and informed him, "God told me to call you about the money you owe me and release the debt."

He immediately responded, "I was just thinking about that the other day. I am planning on starting to pay you. I'll send you something soon."

"Uh—did you hear what I said?" I replied.

"You said God told you to call in your debts."

I thought to myself, "I wish that were the case." "No," I replied, "I am calling to tell you I have released you from what you owe me. You don't have to pay me anything anymore." The words were painful as they came out of my mouth.

"Oh! Okay! Thanks! Great!"

Now onto caller number two: "I was calling to tell you that I am canceling the debt you owe me."

"Oh, no! I want to pay you," she responded. "I just haven't been able to yet. But I am going to pay you!"

After hesitating for a second, I told her, "No, seriously, God told me to release your debt. You don't owe me anything." When I was done making phone calls, I thought to myself, "So this is what it feels like to have no one owe me anything." Although I wasn't exactly sure how to describe what *this* felt like.

Earlier in the week, the Lord had impressed upon my heart to go to Sunday morning services at a church in the next town. Since my car was celebrating Christmas early by flashing an array of lights signaling everything from engine to oil, I decided to get a ride. So after obediently canceling my debts I called to confirm my transportation. When I hung up, I thought, "With all God has had me release today, He must have something special for me tomorrow."

I was hoping I would get some revelation during worship the following morning, but since I was having trouble concentrating, much less receiving, I began to question: "God, I know I was supposed to come here today, but why?"

About that time, a lady walked down to the front of the church. She began to share her testimony about how God had answered prayers and blessed her with another computer. Apparently, the church had prayed for God to bring her a computer when hers had crashed. What she said next literally changed my life: "I need a computer because I'm an editor. She then paused and looked out over the congregation. "There is someone here today who is supposed to write a book. God says, 'Get busy!'"

Although I wrote a good portion of this book in 2008, I had been stumped for the last two years. Each time I tried to revise it I became frustrated, feeling as if I were lost in an endless sea of words. About a month before that Sunday I had cried out to God, "If you want me to finish this book then you need to send me an editor!" Could this be the answer to my prayers? It ends up it was. That day I met Jan after the service. She became my first editor when she offered to edit my book—possibly books—for a donation or nothing. What a blessing she has been!

I once heard a woman say in reference to cleaning out her daughter's closet: "My daughter knows she can't get new clothes until she gets rid of what doesn't fit her." Sometimes I think that it's the same with God. I can just hear Him saying: "I have things I want you to do, but you can't move forward until you get rid of what you are hanging on to." Releasing my debts, released my security and moved me into yet another season of trusting God—not just to supply all my needs, but also to open new doors of opportunity. And what a wonderful season it was, as I enjoyed my adorable grandchildren, wrote more of this book, and witnessed God do some amazing things in the lives of some very precious military wives!

♥ Heart Encounter ♥

1. Before I could receive the blessing and encouragement of an editor God had me release my debts. Is there anyone who "owes" you?

2. There have been times when I have been led to hold people accountable for fulfillment of financial obligations or unwise or harmful actions. But, at other times, I have been led to just grant mercy and give favor. The key is to know and do what is best in each individual situation. Have you ever asked God what will both bring Him the greatest glory, and you, as well as others, the greatest freedom, when someone is indebted to you?

3. In Matthew 18:21-35, Jesus tells the story of a man who was released of a huge debt only to go and demand the small debt that another owed him. Can you relate? I can. However, as I read the story, it's not the financial debts I think about. It's the debts from wounds. What are some of the wounds that have been inflicted on you or your loved ones because of the actions of others?

4. When someone hurts our family or hurts us, we want them to either repay us or to pay a price for what they have done. Although that does happen, I have discovered the majority of the time—it does not. Are you holding onto debts owed to you or to a loved one because of abuse, neglect, deception, betrayal, or abandonment? If so, what are they? Are you ready to trust God and release those debts?

When I was going through my divorce, God gave me a vision of a treasure chest filled with note card-sized pieces of paper. When I asked the Lord what it meant, He told me, *"Those are IOU's you have written to yourself and the kids from Joe."* He then told me to turn to Matthew 18:21-35. After reading the account of the servant who was forgiven of much, God told me, *"I have released your debts. Release the IOU's. Joe owes you nothing. It was all paid for on Calvary! He owes you nothing."* Although I was still supposed to hold Joe accountable for child support, etc., God was telling me that I was not to expect him to pay us back for all the pain he had caused us. I have to admit, though, releasing these debts was not easy or instant; especially when they continued to accrue.

It's human nature to want repayment for pain. Somehow, we think if a price was paid, we wouldn't hurt anymore—or in some cases *be* hurt anymore. But the truth is, even if we could receive payment, the deeds of men are not capable of healing the hurts of the heart. Removing the IOU's from our treasure chests and nailing them to the cross, releases us from the hold of the enemy and opens our spirits to receive the Lord's healing—which was *also* already paid for at Calvary

Let's Pray:

Sweet Jesus, thank you for paying for all of my debts on Calvary. Not just the debts I owe, but the debts that are owed to me. I choose to release those who have hurt my family and myself by nailing the *IOU's* to the cross. Come and heal my heart and restore my soul. In Jesus' Name…Amen!

Reflections:

_____

_____

_____

_____

_____

_____

_____

_____

Revisiting the Broken Places

A few months ago, a late night phone call set off a course of events that challenged me, sending me on a detour into a season of extreme change. Due to meningitis and pneumonia, my mother had been air-vacced to San Antonio and was on life support. Within 48 hours, I was flying out for her funeral—or so I thought.

Although it was *touch and go* for almost two weeks, mom miraculously recovered from her initial ailments. I rode with her via ambulance back to Corpus Christi, where she was temporarily placed in a skilled nursing unit. But the drama was far from over.

Over the course of the next two months, Mom almost died numerous times. Not only had she developed a life-threatening bacterial infection from all of the antibiotics, she was diagnosed with congestive heart failure. She also had some severe reactions to meds, suffered infections, and even hemorrhaged. She was placed on life support two more times. When the doctors gave her no hope, God intervened in such a miraculous way she not only totally woke up, but immediately began breathing on her own saying, "God has things for me to do!" That is the day my daughter nicknamed her Grandma Lazarus.

During my visit I became Mom's advocate and often her nurse, which meant hand-feeding her and sometimes sleeping on floors or in chairs at whatever hospital or care center she was in at the time. I also did secretarial work for Dad and helped care for my special needs sister. Needless to say, I was stretched and often exhausted.

Thankfully, the Lord gave me reprieves through some wonderful brothers and sisters in Christ. Sometimes I was "stolen away" for a church service, dinner, a walk, or movie. At other times, both Mom and I were ministered to at various facilities. All in all, I was amazed how the Lord supplied all my needs, financial, physical, and emotional—even the need for someone to comfort me during a total meltdown one afternoon. In the midst of being poured out and poured into, the Lord brought me much more restoration.

Near the end of my Texas visit, I woke up one morning hearing: *"Revisit the broken places."* For a while I had felt that I needed to go to a certain house in town and pray. Now, I knew that I was not only to go to *that* house, but a few others. They were all places where childhood wounds were inflicted. Just the day before, when my friend Lakendra was praying for me, she said that God told her I needed more healing from my childhood. I remember telling her, "I already have received healing from my childhood. If you only knew *how much* healing I have had! I can't think of anything else I need healing for!"

When I began to share with Lakendra some of the emotional healing I had received because of wrong choices I made when I was young (mainly from being exposed to pornography) she interjected, "How old were you?"

"Seven to ten—but I knew better! I know God has forgiven me," I replied.

"First of all," said Lakendra, "I'm not sure if God holds you accountable at that age, and secondly, don't you think the parents had some responsibility for children accessing porn?" I had never thought about that before. Had I been carrying a burden that was not mine to carry for almost forty-two years?

Lakendra then began speaking to me about *Little Jeannie*, the little girl I'd been when I was exposed to pornography: "The adult Jeannie now knows the truth about God's love, forgiveness, and healing," said Lakendra, "but *Little Jeannie* does not. *Little Jeannie* is still carrying guilt and shame. God wants to heal *Little Jeannie*." I told Lakendra that I would do whatever it took to be healed, but I was frustrated because I had no idea what that would be. So when the Lord woke me and told me to re-visit the broken places—actual places where I had experienced trauma and pain in my childhood—I knew He was showing me the next step. I was then led to read about the rebuilding of the wall in Jerusalem in the book of Nehemiah. After reading the first six chapters, I called a friend and asked if he would go with me when I visited some of the places where I had been broken as a child.

A few nights later, as my friend and I stood outside certain homes and prayed, I asked God to show me *His* truth in each situation. As I walked back and forth declaring restoration, old memories flooded my mind. Instead of just seeing people, I saw plans—plans of the enemy. I became more aware of how the enemy had set traps to destroy me by causing me to believe lies about my value, my identity, and my purpose. That night, as I laid down more of my burdens and took up more truth, I felt both lighter and freer.

Looking back, I realize that God was bringing me restoration the entire time I was in Texas. Besides the restoration I received from visiting the broken places, I received more healing and restoration with my father, my sister, and many other family members. Some of that restoration came through an impromptu family reunion where I got to see cousins I hadn't seen in thirty and forty years. There were many *do overs*—same places, same people—different results. Although some of the restoration came easily, other parts required patience, perseverance, and lots and lots of prayer. But thankfully, because of God's love and faithfulness *Little Jeannie* received more freedom and healing, and the Lord rebuilt more of the *broken places* in my life.

♥ *Heart Encounter* ♥

1. Since we live in an imperfect world and are surrounded by imperfect people, all of us have been broken in some way. Whether it's through hurtful words or hurtful actions, the plans the enemy set in place to destroy us caused us to believe some lies about God, ourselves, and others. Can you think of some lies that you believed, or may still believe, as a result of being hurt?

2. The morning God told me to revisit the broken places, He led me to read about the rebuilding of the wall of Jerusalem in the book of Nehemiah. The Israelites were conquered by their enemies because of their sin and rebellion against God. Although the adults committed the sins, the children were taken into captivity as well. Much of our childhood brokenness results from the choices of others. Although you and I can't go back and erase the circumstances, we can allow God to bring restoration from the consequences.

What are some of the broken places from your childhood?

3. When Nehemiah and the people began to rebuild, they hit major opposition. So much opposition they had to work with a tool in one hand and a weapon in the other. Since the devil doesn't want us to be free, he will oppose us when God has us revisit the broken places in our lives. In the process of restoration you and I must be willing to fight, using the weapons of God's Word, revelation of the Holy Spirit, and prayer, while building with the tools of wise counsel. Whether our wise counsel comes from pastors, professional counselors, books, classes, or friends—or a combination of these, you and I must do the hard work and put forth the effort to rebuild. Have you received wise counsel concerning your broken places? Why or why not?

4. To re-visit means that we have to go back to somewhere—or to someone we've visited in the past. For many years, I clung to the part of Philippians 3:13 that says, "forgetting those things which are behind and reaching forward to those things which are ahead." I interpreted this to mean "Don't ever think about or deal with anything in your past." The only problem, was my unhealed past was affecting my

present relationships and actions. God had to reveal to me that my unhealed past was like a heavy life-sized dummy with its arms wrapped around my leg. Not only was it constantly with me influencing my everyday life, whenever I took a sweeping step forward, it flopped out in front of me affecting my future. Is your past still affecting your present and consequently, future relationships and choices? Explain.

5. When Jerusalem was finally rebuilt, it was better than it was before. Revisiting and rebuilding the broken places has not only made *me* better, but it also has given me better opportunities to share the Lord with others. When God restores what the enemy has destroyed, He brings forth His greater glory. Are you willing to ask God to help you revisit the broken places so He can bring you restoration for His glory?

The day my friend talked about *Little Jeannie* I thought I had already finished healing from my childhood. I wasn't aware that I was still perceiving some situations through the eyes of a wounded child. Often how you and I perceive circumstances and ourselves as children affects our lives as adults. I can now see that this was the case. What *Adult Jeannie* already knew about God's love, forgiveness, and restoration, *Little Jeannie* still needed revealed in order to be healed. Thankfully, that happened when God met me as I *revisited the broken places.*

Let's Pray:

Precious Lord, Thank you for loving me so much that you desire my restoration and healing. Show me how my past is influencing my relationships and choices. Continue to bring your truth and healing to the broken places in my life so I can receive all you have for me. In Jesus' Name…Amen!

Reflections:

_____
_____
_____
_____
_____
_____
_____
_____

What Is It?

*A*fter learning the definition of manna in college Bible class, I headed with a few of my fellow students to the cafeteria. Upon entering the kitchen, we amused ourselves immensely as we pointed to the various indescribable creations while repeating, "Look! Manna!" (Please keep in mind that we were freshman!)

I'm not sure if the cafeteria women thought that we were insinuating their concoctions were heavenly, or if they just thought that we were insane, but they obviously were ignorant concerning our "little joke." For unbeknownst to them, every time we said the word *manna* we were referring to its definition—what is it? Come to think of it, that could also describe some of the dishes *I* have come up with at times!

It makes sense that the Israelites named manna "What is it?" because its appearance and texture was foreign to them. But their lack of familiarity and maybe ingenuity, did not change the fact that every morning as they rose to gather their daily supply (except before the Sabbath when they were led to gather a double portion), their "What is it" was waiting for them to provide sustenance and strength for the day.

At the onset of my divorce, my lawyer assured me that my case would be finalized in three months. However, upon approaching the one-year mark, not only had it become apparent that I was going to have to hang in for the *long haul*, I also wondered why I had been blessed with the slowest lawyer on the face of the earth.

With each passing day, I became more anxious and often would reach for the phone to call my "turtle lawyer" to urge him to accelerate the process. But invariably God would gently tell me to put down the receiver and trust Him. My comprehension of this new aspect of trust, which I definitely was failing at, defied my definition of common sense and hindered me from being able to "get on with my life."

Now you have to realize, that to me, "getting on with my life" meant that I not only was expecting God to give me immediate direction, but I also wanted Him to provide me with a five-year plan for my future—complete with bold headings and outlines.

One morning, when I was worrying about future decisions, such as moving, schooling, and career choices, I was reminded that in the book of Exodus, the Israelites were supplied with a *daily* portion of manna. The Lord then impressed upon my heart that I too could trust Him to daily supply *my* needs. And He did!

My manna came in different forms. Sometimes, it appeared physically as in clothes, money, or groceries left at my door. At other times, it came through scriptures and insight given by others or impressed upon my heart. I was never left lacking. Often, my manna came as specific instructions: *"Today, you are to find out the trade in value on your car." "Today, you are to call a realtor." "Today, you are to just spend time with your children." "Today, you are to take your children to McDonald's."* (I'm not kidding about the last one either. Maybe I'll share that story in my next book.)

Daily waiting on God for my manna taught me to trust God more and to be less fearful. In Philippians 4 the Word tells us that we are not to be anxious for *anything*. **Anything** is a *very* broad term! I'm still working on that one. Although I might not have mastered all my anxiety, I have discovered that when I lay down my fears and choose to *daily* trust the Lord, I have a lot less confusion and a whole lot more peace.

♥ *Heart Encounter* ♥

1. We are reminded in Lamentations 3:21-23 that the Lord's mercies and compassion are new every morning, and His faithfulness is great. Although each morning I might not be gathering a basketful of honey-flavored wafers, I can open up the basket of

my heart and receive my daily portion of "manna" as I go before the Lord asking *"What is it* that you have for me today?" Are you daily opening your heart to receive from the Lord? Explain.

2. Whether my daily portion is a helping of strength, grace, and peace, or whether it is a revelation of things I need to know or change, God always has just what I need. What do you need today?

3. Although God has so much to "give us," fear will sometimes keep us from receiving. In Philippians 4:6-7 we are given step by step instructions to combat anxiousness. I have learned when I follow these guidelines by praying and having a thankful heart, instead of worrying, I have peace. Are you making your requests to God with a thankful heart?

4. I love verse 4:7 in this passage of Philippians! God's peace "which surpasses all understanding, will guard your hearts and minds through Christ Jesus." Have you ever experienced God's peace that "transcends *ALL* understanding?" How can this kind of peace guard your heart?

When you and I lay down our fears and give thanks, we not only receive peace "beyond all understanding," our hearts are also prepared to receive our daily manna. Even though we may not always know whether our manna will come in the form of revelation, provision, or instruction, because of God's incredible love for us, we can be assured that it will always be *precisely* what we need.

Let's Pray:

Dear Lord, Thank you for the blessings in my life. Bring me more revelation of who you are and what you want me to learn and do. I receive your peace that "transcends all understanding." Guard my heart and mind and keep my spirit open to receive my daily portion of manna from you. In Jesus' Name….Amen!

Reflections:

_____
_____
_____
_____
_____
_____
_____
_____
_____

The Red Sea

*A*s I knelt on the floor of my room I could almost feel the mist on my face. It was as if I had been transported to another place, another time. God was telling me that it was time to cross over and head towards the promised land of Canaan. He had already delivered me from my Egypt. But despite all of Egypt's misery and pain, I was being held back because the familiar still felt safer to me than the unknown.

Every time I was fearful or lonely, I would forget the reality of where I had come from and beg God to let me go back. "It really wasn't that bad," I would try to convince myself, "Please let me try again!" It was in those times that the Lord would gently but firmly encourage me: *"I delivered you from Egypt. Why would you want to go back?"* Then He would graciously remind me how it *really* was, squelching my longing for Egypt until my next vulnerable moment.

As I stayed on my knees, the living vision continued

to play out around me. The Egyptian army was rapidly approaching. I stood looking out at the expanse of the waters before me. How could I ever cross over? God was calling me to do something utterly ridiculous—utterly impossible! He was calling me to a new place—a radical place—a place of complete relational and financial dependence on Him. And I was terrified!

Just moments before, I had been led to read the biblical account in Exodus that relates what transpired after the Israelites left Egypt. In Exodus 13:17-18, we read that God deliberately took the Israelites on an unfamiliar route—the way of the wilderness, "Lest perhaps the people change their minds when they see war, and return to Egypt." The Lord then spoke to my heart that He had been taking me by an unfamiliar wilderness way for the same reason. He had now brought me to the place where I stood between my enemies and an impossibility—the Red Sea!

I turned and faced my foes. As they continued to approach with a vengeance, I could hear the hoof beats of the horses, the whirl of the chariot wheels, and the war cries of the soldiers. The approaching army was no longer Pharaoh's army, it was now an army of *my* personal enemies. I was paralyzed. My mind and heart had been tormented for so long. I feared that these cruel taskmasters of my soul that bore the names of guilt, condemnation, insecurity, fear, doubt, loneliness, abuse, and so many others would finally overtake me. There was no hope for me, shy of a miracle. Only God could make a way where there was no way and take me to the *promised land—the land flowing with milk and honey!*

My Heavenly Father had brought me to this place, at this time, to be part of something terrifying—yet wonderful. I stood in awe as the waters began to roll back and part before me. Then I reluctantly took my first step toward the freedom of complete dependence on God. As my foot landed on dry ground I realized that before the beginning of time, my loving Father had prepared this path for me. It had just been concealed until now.

As I cautiously began walking forward, I found myself in a dichotomy. Although I was in awe of the miracle that surrounded me, I was terrified that at any moment the walls of water that encompassed me would suddenly come crashing down, sending me to a watery grave. At times, I didn't know which I feared more—my mercenaries or the miracle.

With each new step I battled: "How did I know that I could trust the heart of God? Were His intentions toward me really toward good and not evil, or was He just setting me up? Was the Lord actually taking me to the other side? Was the promised Canaan an authentic place or just a fairy tale? And if Canaan was really a place of abundance and freedom then why was God allowing my enemies to follow me into the sea? Why did it seem that He was making a way for them as well?" The farther I walked, the harder they pursued. Was I ever to be free?

The morning God surrounded me with the vision of the Red Sea, He gave me the courage to leave my Egypt behind for good and walk into a season of seeing His faithfulness in the midst of impossibilities. During my journey, I learned that God's heart was truly for me and not against me. Although it took a long time, when I finally did reach the opposite shore of trust, I got to witness firsthand the promise that God gave the Israelites through Moses thousands of years ago: "Do not be afraid. Stand still, and see the salvation of the Lord, which He will accomplish for you today. For the Egyptians whom you see today, you shall see again no more forever" (Exodus 14:13).

As I witnessed the cascading waters that I feared would engulf me, come crashing down and annihilate the tormentors of my soul, I once again was reminded that the Israelites are not remembered for their great faith— instead they are remembered for the faithfulness of their *great God!* And just like Moses and the children of Israel, after they witnessed the destruction of the Egyptians thousands of years before, my soul rejoiced shouting, "I will sing to the Lord, For He has triumphed gloriously! The horse and its rider He has thrown into the sea!" (Exodus 15:1).

♥ *Heart Encounter* ♥

1. Do you have an Egypt? Is there a place of bondage that is so familiar to you that you keep trying to run back to it? If so, what is it?

2. Whenever the Israelites felt threatened or pressed they would began to remember all of the good things that they had left behind. The reality is that they forgot how bad life really was for them in Egypt. At times, I have done the same. Have you ever forgotten the grief that God has rescued you from when you face difficulties or are looking into the unknown?

3. The fear of the unknown can keep us from crossing the sea and seeing our enemies destroyed. It can also keep us from feasting on the promises of God. Has the fear of the unknown ever held you back, or caused you to return to the place from which you were rescued? If so, how?

4. Read Exodus chapters 13:17-18. Do you want to continue to run back to a place of bondage or are you willing to let your loving Father take you a different way (*The Way of the Wilderness*) until He brings you

to the impossible place where your faith is challenged, your enemies are destroyed, and His glory is revealed (*The Red Sea*)?

5. The Israelites left Egypt as slaves, but they crossed into Canaan as sons and daughters of God. Are you still living in a slave mentality? If so, what is keeping you there?

6. I am so thankful that through the blood of Jesus Christ you and I are sons and daughters instead of slaves. But we are not just ordinary sons and daughters. We are children of royalty—*princes* and *princesses.* How does knowing that you are a *King's Kid* change the way you see yourself or the promises to which you are entitled?

7. As a *Child of the King*, God has more for you than you can ever think or imagine. But in order to obtain His promises, you must learn to trust Him when He takes you through the way of the Wilderness to the shores of the Red Sea. The question is not, "Are you ready to cross?" The question is "Are you prepared to witness a miracle?!"

Lately I have been going through another Red Sea season. But this time, instead of being fearful I have peace, because I know in my heart that God is for me and not against me. As the Lord continues to take you and me to new lands of promise, we will have seas to cross and Canaans to conquer for the rest of our lives. Thankfully, we can be assured that no matter who our adversaries are or what our circumstances look like, God will make a way where there is no way when He hems us in between our enemies and an impossibility. As God's precious children, we can take heart in these words that were spoken to the Israelites: "…Do not be afraid. Stand still and see the salvation of the Lord…" (Exodus 14:13).

Let's Pray:

Dear Lord, thank you that as your child, through the miracle of the cross, Canaan is mine. Thank you for rescuing me from Egypt. Remind me of the truth of its destruction and bondage if I ever ponder going back. I thank you for taking me ways I have never gone before so as to hem me in between my enemies and impossibilities. In parting the Red Seas in my life, you not only make a way where there is no way, you destroy my foes in the process. Lord, bring glory to your name, as you move mightily in ways beyond man's comprehension, and continue to bring great victories in the impossible situations of my life. In Jesus' Name…Amen!

Reflections:

_____
_____
_____
_____
_____
_____
_____
_____

The Flow

*E*very two years Aglow International has an international conference in which Christians from over two hundred nations come together in one accord to worship and get encouraged in the Word. The first time I was blessed to attend was in Phoenix, Arizona in 1991. The experience still resonates with me. It was like a taste of heaven as sisters in Christ, and even some brothers, lifted their voices and hearts in unity. It wasn't about races, nationalities, backgrounds, or socio-economic statuses. It was just about Jesus—one body, one voice, one purpose—to glorify our risen Savior and prepare us for the destinies He has created for us. Although I would have loved to have gone each time the convention rolled around, the opportunity did not arise for me again until 2006, when a loved one offered to pay for convention costs and plane tickets if my daughters and I wanted to go.

Since our flights had been provided for and I was able

to take vacation from work, I thought everything else would fall into place quite easily. But as our take–off time approached there was still a "little" obstacle standing in our way. We didn't have any traveling money. One morning as I was getting ready for work, I was led to read the story of the loaves and fishes. As I was reading, the Lord spoke to my heart: *"You go; I'll bring the flow."*

During the following month, as I booked our flights and proceeded with the "go," I had yet to see the "flow." I thought all that was going to change a week before departure when a Christian brother took me to lunch and asked me if I had any needs. "Yes, finally, Lord!" I inwardly rejoiced. But before I could spout off my list, the Lord strongly impressed on my heart not to mention the trip. It was definitely one of those "Seriously, Lord?!" moments. As I sat at the table biting my lip knowing that this brother would have willingly provided our necessary food money, I also wondered how my girls would handle the Tennessee snow since they had outgrown their jackets.

The night before departure I sat in my room praying and trying to figure out if I had misheard God. I still didn't have money for gas to get to the airport much less trip expenses. As I was praying for an answer, a man I had been dating called and asked if he could take us to the airport. I immediately accepted his offer, but I didn't feel to mention our lack of funds.

The next morning as my daughters fought over who

would get the window seat on the plane during our two hour drive to the airport, God promised me that we would have what we needed before we arrived in Tennessee.

"Hmmm. Maybe God is going to bless us with the money through my boyfriend," I reasoned. But when we said our goodbyes and he drove away, I was still penniless, and I might also add, a bit bewildered.

Even though I had yet to see the answer to our financial situation, I did see an immediate answer to my daughters' ongoing quarrel as to who would get the window seat on the plane. I must have laughed for five minutes when we sat down in our assigned seats on the windowless back row next to the restroom. (Did I mention that we got a great price on our tickets?) At least we were all together.

However, during the next leg of our journey, that was about to change. When we received our boarding passes during our layover in Dallas, I discovered that our seats had not only been changed, but that we were all in different sections of the plane. As I approached the lady at the desk with the intention of correcting the mix-up, the Lord spoke to my heart: *"Trust me when I change your seats."* So I stepped out of line and sat back down.

While I was explaining the changes to my daughters I noticed a man sitting across the room. Have you ever looked at someone and felt instantly connected to them? I felt so drawn to this man I thought for sure maybe we had gone to school together. But since I couldn't place him and didn't want to stare, I decided to just quietly pray for him.

I also prayed for my daughters before we boarded. A short while later we were waving to each other from our assigned seats. As the rest of the passengers boarded, I continued to wonder who was going to sit in the seat next to me. Just when I thought it would remain empty, the last passenger stepped into view and came and sat down. It was the man I had prayed for in the airport.

Shortly after take-off, the Holy Spirit impressed on my heart that I was to ask him if he knew Jesus as his Lord and Savior. He did. Almost two hours later, after he had shared his story, and I had shared testimonies, and prayed for him, he asked if he could give me some money. "Only if God leads you," I replied. To which he answered, "When I first sat down, I felt I was supposed to give you money." He then handed me $180. I was so excited, I was beside myself—excited to have the much needed cash and also excited that once again God had gone before and fulfilled His promise!

The Lord continued to bless the girls and me with an incredible rest of the day, including finding jackets that were on clearance for $20 each. We also had the privilege of sharing our blessings with a precious little black grandma who brightened our world as she danced around shouting, "Praise Jesus!" after she accepted the money God led us to give her.

Later that night, a Christian brother from my singles group called. "I am so sorry I missed you!" he said. "For two weeks God kept telling me to give you money before you left for your trip. When I went by your house today and found out you had already gone, I didn't know what to do. Did you have enough?" After reassuring him not to worry I told him how God had provided through the man on the plane. My friend then informed me that there would be a check waiting for me when I got home. Wow God! Could it get any better?

That weekend my daughters and I received the gifts of God's presence, power, and provision in so many ways, I have yet to recount them all. I have never felt so spoiled as the Lord continually honored His promise and confirmed that when He tells us to go—He provides the flow!

♥ *Heart Encounter* ♥

1. In John 6:1-15, Jesus used five loaves and two fish to feed over 5,000 people. I wonder what the little boy who gave his five loaves and two fish was thinking. Do you think he was trying to figure out why Jesus wanted his lunch, or did he just give it willingly, because he wanted Jesus to have it? Do you willingly give your time, talents, and finances when Jesus asks, or do you, like me, sometimes play 20 questions with God when He asks you to give Him something or to trust Him? Explain.

2. Sometimes you and I can get so caught up in trying to figure out the whys that we forget a simple act of obedience comes from a "childlike" faith. What does the scripture, "Come as a little child" mean to you?

3. The gift of the loaves and the fishes were the "go." How did Jesus provide the "flow?"

4. Is God challenging you to step out in faith and give Him your "loaves and fishes"? If so, how?

Not only was the giver blessed in giving what he had, but thousands were blessed as a result. As God calls us to *go* He will bring forth a greater *flow* than we can imagine. The flow of finances, the flow of peace, the flow of testimony, the flow of His presence, the flow that could touch thousands of lives as you and I share the amazing things He has done in and through us. Just *GO*, my friend! And *He* will do the rest.

Let's Pray:

Sweet Jesus, I choose to trust you with my life, my heart—"my lunch." Help me to step out in childlike faith and trust that you will provide the flow when I go. I will go where you tell me to go. I will say what you tell me to say, I will do what you tell me to do. Lord, it's all about you. Take the little I have and multiply it to touch the lives of many. In Jesus' Name…Amen!

Reflections:

_____

_____

_____

_____

_____

_____

_____

_____

_____

911

"*I* could rape you right now and no one would hear you!"

How did it come to this?! When Jamie told me he could sneak me into his dorm to study, I really planned on studying. But almost immediately after we sat down at his desk, he whisked me off the chair and tossed me on the bed. I sat up and kissed him for a few minutes, then pushed him away and got back into the chair. "Now remember, Jamie," I said in a laughing tone. "We are supposed to be studying." He wasn't laughing.

A few minutes later, he again scooped me up and put me back on the bed, I began to get concerned. When he asked me for a sexual favor, I was shocked that this blonde-headed, blue-eyed preacher's kid with the angelic face would even suggest such a thing. I calmly replied, "Jamie, I'm not that type of girl."

"I heard your friend Denise does it," he countered.

"Well I'm not Denise!" I shot back.

"Come on, nothing is wrong with it. Lots of girls do it," he coaxed. "Just last week I had a gal up here and she didn't have a problem with it."

When I again told him "No," both his facial expression and body language began to change. "I don't know what is wrong with me," he voiced, "Why do I do these things? What is wrong with me?!"

"Nothing is wrong with you," I reassured him. Although I wanted to believe what I had told him, his increased agitation was freaking me out, so I gathered my things and headed toward the door. That is when Jamie overpowered me and pinned me to the floor.

You are probably wondering how any college sophomore could be so naïve. Not only was I naive, but up until that afternoon, I thought I was kind of invincible. As long as I was wearing my cowboy boots and had my wits about me, I could walk down the darkest alley at the earliest morning hours and feel safe because I had rehearsed my "getaway." Over and over again, I had thought about what I would say and do if a stranger attacked me. But this wasn't a rehearsal, Jamie wasn't a stranger, and I wasn't as strong as I thought. I had never felt so vulnerable. I couldn't even move my legs, much less kick the "Bible major" off of me!

On our first date, Jamie had mentioned a campus newspaper article about a recent date rape at our small Christian college. "And the guy was a *Bible* major! Can you believe that?" he exclaimed.

Up to that moment I almost couldn't. But as I was

pinned to floor being told how thick the walls were, how vacant the building was, and how weak I was, being violated by a Bible major was not only a possibility, it was a probability.

"I could rape you right now and no one would know," he sneered.

His words incited fear—fear like I have never experienced before. Fear that told me that I was weak and defenseless—fear that shook me to the core of my being.

I don't remember if I prayed actual words that afternoon, but someone dialed heaven's 911. Because what came out of my mouth, did not reflect what was in my quivering soul. "Oh, that would make you a real man, wouldn't it?!" I stated with a volume and firmness that even surprised me. "Yeah, that would really prove you're a man!" As I finished the words, Jamie released my wrists and pushed off of me. I got up—still shaken but determined not to show it, went into the restroom and defiantly put on my lipstick and left.

My insides continued to quiver as I made my way across campus feeling both violated and foolish. As I approached my dorm room I could hear my phone ringing. After hurriedly turning the key, I swung the door open and snatched the receiver off the wall phone next to the door. It was my mother. Her voice was like music to my ears. "Jeannie, what is going on? She anxiously inquired. "I felt led to pray for you. Are you Okay?"

Yep, someone had dialed 911.

♥ *Heart Encounter* ♥

1. I could write a book simply on the divine interventions I have seen because of the prayers of my "praying mama." Not only in the incident with Jamie, but in many other situations. Since Mom always seemed to *know* when I or another one of my siblings was in trouble "Is anything wrong?" and "I felt led to pray" became familiar phrases in my family. For years I wondered what my mother's special gift was all about—until I became a mother. Love will definitely motivate us to "hit our knees" for our loved ones. Have the prayers of a righteous man or woman impacted your life? Explain.

2. Although I have talked to many people who have acknowledged answers to prayers, occasionally I meet someone who has said that no one ever prayed for them. I tell them there is a good chance someone *was* praying, even if they were unaware. Then I share some of the times when I was led to pray for neighbors and strangers without them ever knowing. You never know whose heart God is stirring to pray for you, or for whom God might put on your heart to pray. Read Acts 12:5. Do you think Peter *knew* the Christians at Lydia's house were "praying for him?" What was the result of *their* prayers?

3. I mentioned before that my mother always seemed to know when we were in trouble. Through the years I saw her answer a lot of 911 calls from God's intercession switchboard—prayers for her children and for others. Mom was an incredible intercessor, but I don't necessarily believe it was Mom's anointing that allowed God to entrust her with so much. It was her availability. For Mom stayed on call 24/7. Are you on call? Do you keep an attitude of praying without ceasing?

I learned a lot from Mom about prayer, and I too have tried to stay "available." Whether it's mid-night intercession that has jarred me out of a sound sleep, or daily intervention that has caused me to drop to my knees, I have learned to continue to pray until I feel a release. On numerous occasions, I have been blessed to see and hear the results of my petitions. But even when I haven't, I could always be assured that Heaven's switchboard was buzzing, because someone called 911.

Let's Pray:

Dear Lord, thank you for the hearts you have stirred to pray for me, even when I have not been aware. I choose to be a part of what you are doing by praying for others. Keep my spiritual ears open so I can be "on call" for your Kingdom purposes. Bring forth your glory through answered prayers! In Jesus' Name…Amen!

Reflections:

_____
_____
_____
_____
_____
_____
_____
_____
_____

From Fear to Faith

When my oldest son Joshua was two years old, I took him to the beach with some of my siblings and their children. As soon as Joshua got out of the car he bolted across the sand toward the water. I took off after him, scooped him up in my arms and told him he couldn't go in the water without me. My sister-in-law then got in his face and said, "Joshua, do you see that water? If you go in the water, it will take you away and you will *never* come back!" Well, that did the trick. Even a stampeding herd of elephants wouldn't have been able to get Joshua into those "child eating" waves.

Instead of Joshua "having faith" that he was safe in the water if he was with me, my sister-in-law's words terrified my son so much, that whenever a wave would wash up within 10 feet of us, he would run to me screaming, attach himself to my leg, and attempt to climb me like a tree. Needless to say, our "day at the beach" wasn't a very pleasant experience.

Although my sister-in-law had good intentions, her fear reaction brought about undesirable results. At times, my "fear reactions" have also done the same. Once when my preschool daughter Shanna picked up a spray bottle of bleach, instead of calmly approaching her and taking the bottle from her and explaining the contents could hurt her, I shouted, "Don't touch that! It can kill you!" as I leapt across a chair and ripped it from her hands. As a result, she became terrified of anything in a bottle for the next few years. She also began what became years of continuous hand washing.

In the cases of both my son and daughter, fear birthed more fear, but fear can also contribute to other undesirable outcomes. A few years ago, God really began to deal with my heart about the importance of acting from the place of faith, instead of reacting from the place of fear, not just in my daily walk with Him but in my relationships with others. One of the examples He showed me was how I had monitored my children's movie time. Whenever I had caught my children watching graphic violence or nudity, I had a habit of gasping, running to the TV, and covering the screen with a pillow until the scene was over. The "faith way" would have been to calmly walk over and say, "Remember our agreement? This show does not meet the criteria to which we agreed. Reacting in fear only incited their curiosity, which was definitely *not* my desired goal.

The more I have become aware of the consequences of being motivated by fear, the more I have purposed to be proactive (the way of faith) instead of reactive (the way of fear) when making moral stands, confronting situations, or deciding life choices.

For example: If I have a need, being proactive would mean expressing my need to the Lord, praying for wisdom, and trusting that God will supply. Trusting God could mean a financial miracle, extra hours of work, or even asking for help. It's up to God how He wants to provide. Reactive would be calling everyone for money or frantically running around looking for extra income. I have tried both ways and God's way far exceeds the way of fear.

If I have a relational conflict, being proactive would mean praying and asking God for wisdom and then calmly, and sometimes firmly, confronting within the guidelines of healthy boundaries. Past experiences have taught me that if I do not have pre-established boundaries, I will usually react in fear. Whether my reactions stem from the fear of not being understood, the fear of being taken advantage of, or the fear of the loss of relationship, they will always yield undesirable results.

Learning to step out in faith instead of reacting in fear has changed my perspective in situations and in relationships, but it has also changed *me*. Since "perfect love casts out fear," in choosing the "faith way" I have been able to experience a greater understanding of God's love for myself and for others, and I've also been blessed with a whole lot more peace.

♥ *Heart Encounter* ♥

1. Although warning and guiding our children is an act of faith, we can do it in a way that incites fear. This happened often when I was growing up. Consequently, I became extremely fearful. Have you ever become fearful as a result of another's fear?

2. Many times our initial fears are founded in actual experiences. If we don't allow God to heal us, we can end up developing irrational fears. By the time I was in my twenties I was operating in lots of irrational fear. It took many years and much revelation for me to be set free. Have you ever, or are you now, operating in irrational fear? Explain.

3. Since I often reacted out of fear with my children, some of their responses also became fear-based. As I have learned truth and grown in God's "perfect love that casts out fear" (I John 4:18), I've seen my children begin to do the same. Does your family tend to be more faith-based or fear-based? Does it comfort you to know that the cycle of fear can be broken?

4. One of the scriptures I often quoted as I was praying for freedom from my fear issues was 2 Timothy1:7. It reads: "For God has not given us a spirit of fear, but of power and of love and a sound mind." The more I understand God's love for me, the more I am empowered to overcome fear. How can understanding God's love, walking in His power, and claiming a sound mind (A mind focused on God and anchored in truth) help you to be a person who acts in faith?

Living out of faith instead of fear changes our lives. Not only do *we* change, but our relationship with God and our relationships with others changes. A faith-based life takes back the ground the enemy has stolen from us and from our children. Ground that is restored because of God's perfect love—His amazing, unconditional love which casts out *all* fear!

Let's Pray:

Dear Lord, I claim a sound mind through your love and your power. The more I realize your love for me and your power working in my life, the less I will fear. I desire to be a person who acts in faith. Break fear off of me and bind me to your perfect love (Yourself). In your presence, fear has to leave. I take the authority you have given me through Jesus and command fear to go. Give me your perspective concerning my situations and relationships, and flood my mind and heart with your peace. In Jesus' Name…Amen

Reflections:

_____

_____

_____

_____

_____

_____

_____

_____

_____

Too Fast Too Soon

*W*hen I was eight years old the desire of my heart was a plastic dish set so I could play tea party with my dolls. I wasn't hoping for just any dish set. I had my eye on the Rolls Royce of dish sets, featuring pretty much everything except the kitchen sink. Many an afternoon, you could find me sitting cross-legged with the big mail order catalog draped across my lap salivating (I wonder if mom noticed the drool marks) over the deeply creased page picturing an assortment of miniature place settings—complete with silverware, serving dishes, pots, pans, glasses, and utensils. So imagine my excitement Christmas morning when I not only received one, but *two* of the coveted sets!

After immediately taking ownership of the beautiful blue floral set, I readily agreed to Mom's suggestion to give the second peach tulip dishes to one of the children who came by bus to church. So the following Sunday morning our ride picked us up early, and Mom and I stayed in the car while everyone else went into the sanctuary. The bus usually arrived shortly before service started, but this particular morning it seemed to be taking *forever*. Just when it seemed I could wait no longer I looked up to see its enormous front window staring at me as if it were a gigantic eye peering down and wondering what I was up to.

I firmly clasped the dish set in my hands as I watched the metallic monster pass and park at the side of the building, waiting for it to spill out its contents of captive children. As my eyes anxiously darted back and forth among the youngsters dismounting the steps, I wondered who would be gifted with the present. Within a few minutes, which to my young eagerness seemed like an eternity, I spied a little girl about five or six years old standing alone. I leapt out of the car, ran up to her, and presented her with the dishes. Her eyes lit up as she smiled and thanked me for the gift. Once my delivery had been completed, I ran back to the car where Mom was waiting for me.

As I jumped back into the car to gather up my Bible and purse, I saw another little girl out of the corner of my eye. Her disheveled appearance and slow gait pricked my heart. An inner sadness seemed to permeate her entire being. I immediately knew in my spirit I had acted too impulsively. Without saying a word, I looked over at Mom. She simply smiled at me and said, "You gave them to the wrong girl, didn't you?" I nodded.

I don't remember if Mom and I prayed for God to

bring that little girl a set of dishes for Christmas. Knowing Mom, we probably did. However, the memory of the second little girl was forever etched in my mind, because despite my good intentions, my impatience and eagerness had caused me to jump *too fast and too soon.*

As Christians we have a lot to give. Whether it's physical gifts, or gifts of our time or ministry, it's easy to jump out in our own understanding and give to the wrong person and/or people or even to give at the wrong time. It is certainly God's heart for us to give. We can't out-give Him. But as His vessels, we need to submit our giving and our gifts to Him, trusting that *He* will show us when, where, and how to give.

Not long ago the Lord placed a vision in my heart, and I immediately tried to make it happen. That is when God reminded me that I needed to pray for *His* timing and *His* ways. As we continue to be faithful in the now, without giving up on the vision God has given us, we can be assured that even when it may not seem like it, He is already orchestrating divine circumstances that, in *His* time, will bring those visions to pass.

♥ *Heart Encounter* ♥

1. Have you ever jumped too fast, too soon? If so, what were the results?

2. Sometimes, as in the incident with the dish set, I have jumped ahead and leapt out in my own understanding out of excitement, but at other times, it has solely been from the motivation of pride and/or the approval of man. Have you ever found yourself jumping ahead of God's timing because of pride or the fear of man? If so, how has pride and/or approval affected your decisions?

3. I specifically remember a time when I was striving to prematurely fulfill a vision God had placed on my heart. One night I had a dream in which I was trying to care for a room full of babies on my own. The more I changed and fed the infants, the more care they needed. Finally, in exasperation, I threw up my hands in defeat. When I woke from my dream, the Lord revealed that I had been operating in pride by trying to accomplish the vision on my own. He also showed me that many people would be involved in bringing the vision to pass. Once again, I had to watch out for the "I" factor that was an underlying current in "my plans." Have you ever found yourself being motivated by the "I" factor?

4. The "I" factor takes the good plans of God and moves them into the realm of the flesh. What is about God becomes about us. How are *we* going to accomplish

the vision? What are people going to say about *us*? What recognition are *we* going to receive? Our words and actions begin to revolve around *me me me* instead of *He He He.* In John 7:18 Jesus tells us that "He who speaks from himself seeks His own glory; but He who seeks the glory of the One who sent Him is true, and no unrighteousness is in Him." Can you think of a situation in the past or maybe even in the present where you have proclaimed what *you* have done more than proclaiming what the *Lord* has done in your life? What is the truth?

God is good, loving, merciful, and true, but He will *not* share His glory with another. He won't share His glory, not only because He alone is God, but also because when man is glorified, it brings destruction to himself (man), as well as to others. Just like the Israelites had to drink the melted gold from the golden calf in Exodus 32:20, we will taste the bitterness of whatever we build from the wrong motivations of our hearts. That is why it is wise to keep the words that Paul spoke to the Corinthians in mind, as we move forward in our giving and our giftings *"He who glories, let him glory in the Lord"* (1 Corinthians 1:31).

Let's Pray:

Precious Lord, I know that you have given me gifts and abilities. Show me when, where, and how to share them. Reveal to me the true motivations of my heart as I move forward toward the visions you have shown me. Uncover pride, independence, and any "me" centered roots that would cause me to jump *Too Fast Too Soon*, or to do things in my own understanding. Be glorified in my life and let me glory in you and you alone. In Jesus' Name….Amen!

Reflections:

_____

_____

_____

_____

_____

_____

_____

_____

_____

I'll Get There First

My good friend Bruce and I had an understanding. If I was busy when he called me at work, I would say, "Can't talk," and then I would call him back when I was available. So the afternoon He called me back immediately after I had hung up on him, I was a bit surprised. "Bruce, I said I would call you…" He abruptly stopped me in mid-sentence, "No, Jeannie! Don't hang up! I'm at the hospital. I need you to pray! They think I have cancer!"

Cancer—such a small word with such huge repercussions! I sat in stunned silence with the phone glued to my hand until my boss questioning if I was okay brought me back to reality. "My friend is in the hospital. They think he has cancer," I said. Although the words didn't *seem* real as I said them, they *were* real—*way* too real!

That evening my best friend Albert, who was also my ministry partner, went with me to see Bruce. During our hour drive to the hospital, Albert and I prayed, worshipped, and declared the promises of God. When we arrived, Bruce was still in the emergency room awaiting a bed.

Last time I had seen Bruce he had been talking about making a doctor's appointment because he was having difficulty breathing. He was pale then—but now he was white as a sheet. And no wonder, he had been functioning on only a third of his blood volume. The technician at the hospital said he had never had someone walk into the emergency room, much less drive and hour to get there, with such a low blood count. They had to give him an entire gallon.

That night, as Albert and I stood by Bruce's bed, I heard Bruce first say the statement that would point me toward the eternal in a new way: "I know God can heal me. But if He chooses not to—I'm going to get there first." Over the next few months I heard it often as Bruce received numerous transfusions, went through a myriad of tests, and eventually was blessed with a bone marrow donor. Everyone who knew him was overjoyed when a "match" had been found for him.

Albert and I visited Bruce and prayed for him the night before the transplant. He was so excited! Before I left that night, I once again heard the familiar words that had already given so many people courage and hope, "I know that God can heal me. But if He chooses not to—I'm going to get there first." The next time I heard those words, they were being read at his funeral service.

My friend Bruce left behind a legacy, not as much in *how* He lived, but for *whom* He lived for in the end. Even though he didn't always stay on course when running the race of life, he knew where to cross the finish line.

During Bruce's final months on earth he wholeheartedly ran after the Lord and impacted many lives. I was told he even had a small Bible study at the hospital with some other cancer patients. If anyone, including me, called Bruce to see how he was doing, he would immediately turn the conversation to *their* needs and pray for *them.*

Although, I miss Bruce, I know that someday I will see him again. He might have crossed the finish line and "gotten there first!" but thankfully, through the atoning blood of Jesus, all who receive Christ as Savior will also finish the race and "get there."

♥ *Heart Encounter* ♥

1. 2 Timothy 4:7 says "I have fought the good fight, I have finished the race, I have kept the faith." It's interesting that Paul uses the analogies of both a fight and a race. Although the Holy Spirit gives me much joy, sometimes "keeping the faith" for me has felt more like dodging bullets in a war zone than running a marathon. Can you relate?

2. The following scripture sums up the courage and heart I saw in Bruce as he ran to the finish line: "But none of these things move me; nor do I count my life dear to myself, so that I may finish my race with joy, and the ministry which I received from the Lord Jesus, to testify to the gospel of the grace of God" (Acts 20:24). Do these scriptures give you courage and stir your heart? Making our lives *less* about *us* and *more* about *God* brings us joy and reveals God's love and grace to others. Are you reflecting God's gospel of grace as you "run the race?"

3. 1 Corinthians 9:25 talks about the contrast between perishable and imperishable prizes (or crowns). There is a song that I love that talks about "laying down our crowns." Are there some perishable crowns that you need to lay down? If so, what are they?

4. "Therefore we do not become discouraged (utterly spiritless, exhausted, and wearied out through fear). Though our outer man is [progressively] decaying *and* wasting away, yet our inner self is being [progressively] renewed day by day. For our light, momentary affliction (this slight distress of the passing hour) is ever more abundantly preparing *and* producing *and* achieving for us an everlasting weight of glory [beyond all measure, excessively surpassing

all comparisons and all calculations, a vast and transcendent glory and blessedness never to cease!]" (2 Corinthians 4:16-18 AMP). When all is said and done, only our eternal investments (what we do with and for Jesus) will remain. What heavenly treasures are you storing up?

5. "For now we see in a mirror, dimly, but then face to face. Now I know in part, but then I shall know just as I also am known" (1 Corinthians 13:12). I've often thought when I get to Heaven and see Jesus that I will instantly have answers for all the questions that have troubled me. But lately, I've wondered when I am given a full understanding (knowing Him) and understand the depths of Him knowing me, if I will even care about my questions being answered. What are some of the unanswered questions that have troubled your spirit?

6. As you look into the face of Jesus and are surrounded by the glory of God, do you think having answers concerning life's disappointments is going to matter as much as you thought it would?

The same day Bruce arrived to begin life in eternity, another man Art, who had also been in my singles group, met him. Art was killed in a motorcycle accident within hours of Bruce's death. When I learned of Art's death, I couldn't help but wonder what both of their faces must have looked like when they saw each other. "Praised (honored, blessed) be the God and Father of our Lord Jesus Christ (the Messiah)! By His boundless mercy we have been born again to an ever-living hope through the resurrection of Jesus Christ from the dead" (1 Peter 1:3 AMP).

Sometimes you and I know that death is coming, but sometimes it comes suddenly. The timing is not as important as the condition of our hearts. If you were to die today, is your heart ready? If you have never acknowledged Jesus as your Lord and Savior please pray the following prayer with me. I don't know which one of us is "going to get there first". What's important is that you and I both "get there"!

Let's Pray:

Dear Jesus, Thank you for loving me and dying for my sins. Forgive me and cleanse me. Come into my heart and change my life. I surrender my life to you. I give you my past, my present, and my future. Thank you for being my Savior, my Lord, and my friend. I am excited that I will spend eternity with you! And I look forward to daily walking with you for the rest of my days on this earth. I love you, Jesus! In Your precious and Mighty Name…Amen!

Reflections:

_____
_____
_____
_____
_____
_____
_____
_____
_____

A Lesson from a Gecko

As soon as we had unloaded the car after returning from Christmas vacation, I sat down at the kitchen table with my good friend Greg who had been watching the house during our absence. Just a few sentences into our conversation, we were interrupted by a grievous wail coming from the other room. "Ahhhh! Mooommm, Jimmy is dead!"

My heart immediately went out to my youngest son. Not only was Jimmy the only exception to our landlord's no pet policy, he was also Caleb's best friend. Ever since the day Caleb had stowed his little gecko away in his carry-on during his return flight from visiting his aunt and uncle a few years earlier, Jimmy had daily ridden around on his shoulder.

As Caleb sorrowfully approached the table and continued to lament the loss of his beloved pet, I immediately began to rack my brain as to possible causes of death. All I could come up with was that Jimmy had probably frozen to death, due the small heater in his tank failing to provide him adequate warmth. "I'm sorry, son," I apologized. "I should have left the main heater on low while we were gone. Jimmy probably froze to death." After more tears and a few choruses of "You should have left the heater on! You killed Jimmy!" Caleb ran back into his bedroom sobbing.

Although lack of heat was a logical possibility, something still didn't seem to register so I asked Greg what he thought. "Uhhh—I was *just* going to...tell you about that," Greg slowly replied, "Jimmy was fine up until I came to check on him yesterday. I don't know what could have happened." When I asked Greg if Jimmy had been fed the appropriate serving of meal worms every few days, he assured me he had given him his food on a regular basis. Then, shaking my head in bewilderment, I responded, "I just don't understand. Did he have plenty of water?" The quizzical look on Greg's face said it all before he even spoke: "*Water*? I didn't *know* he needed *water*."

I went to Caleb's room and reluctantly peered into the aquarium on his dresser, His beloved pet gecko was not only lifeless, but statuesque. Jimmy looked as if he had been frozen in time, still in an upright position, with both feet on his small leaf-shaped water dish, his mouth open with his tongue extending downward resting on the rim. It was as if I could hear his last words uttered in the squeaks of his little gecko language, "Thanks for the food and the temperature isn't that bad, but to tell you the truth—I thirst!"

Although Caleb's gecko died of physical dehydration, I can think of times when I have become spiritually dehydrated—even in the midst of comfortable circumstances. Since nothing in this world can satisfy my parched spirit, eventually I become dissatisfied enough to cry out, "I thirst!" and I run to the Word with a renewed zeal. Once I am immersed in the pages of God's love letter, I drink in His presence and He faithfully pours His "Living Water" into my thirsty soul and revives me once again.

♥ Heart Encounter ♥

1. How about you? Do you ever find yourself thirsting for more of the Lord and His truth?

2. Although spiritual dehydration may not cost me my life, it does cost me my peace. Read Psalms 42. Why do you think the writer is comparing himself to a deer in verse 1?

3. Perhaps the deer has been running from a predator. Obviously, it's so thirsty it's panting, which tells us it

is becoming desperate. Have you ever been desperate for more of God? Are you desperate now?

4. Although the writer of this Psalm was obviously suffering in the midst of a very difficult situation, you and I can drink of the deep waters of the Lord in both the good and bad times. When I was younger I was not aware of this, so often my relationship with the Lord resembled more of a panicked person dialing 911. I saw God as being on call when I wanted Him or needed Him, but nothing more. How do you view your relationship with the Lord?

There once was a man I really cared about. The more I communicated with him, the more I desired to know all about him. Since my heart wanted to connect with him, I wanted to not only know his likes and dislikes, I wanted to know all of his life experiences. During that season, the Lord ministered to me that He longed for me to know His heart in the same way.

God doesn't just want you and me to know *about* Him, He wants us to *know* Him. What brings Him joy? What grieves His heart? He wants our lives to be intertwined with the Life in Him, our hearts to beat with His Heart, and our spirits to be moved by His Spirit. As the depth of our spirits connect to depth of whom He is, deep calls unto deep, for surely *we thirst* and our thirst can only be quenched by *His living water.*

Let's Pray:

Sweet Jesus, I want to know you more. I want my heart to beat with your heart. Guide me by your Holy Spirit, and pour your fountains of water into me. Stir up the depths of my soul until I long for you as the deer pants for the water brook. No one but you, Lord, can satisfy my thirst. In Jesus' Name…Amen!

Reflections:

_____

_____

_____

_____

_____

_____

_____

_____

Time to Fly

As I was submitting my first book for publication, I was packing my stuff and putting it in storage—for a season. Once again, God had told me to leave what I knew and fly to a few places, this time to visit family and to minister.

Although Mom had recovered from having meningitis and pneumonia in 2012, she wasn't able to care for herself. So when she was released from the rehabilitation center a few months later, I flew back to Corpus Christi and began caregiving for both her and my special needs sister Judy. I also continued to help my father with his business. That winter my baby brother Mark was diagnosed with cancer.

Mom lived almost two more years. A week before mom went home to be with the Lord, we put her in a hospice unit. Two days before Mother's Day, Mark became non-responsive and we moved him across the hall from Mom. All night long I went back and forth singing to them and praying for them. The Lord's presence and peace was incredible! I even saw angels!

Mark went to heaven the following morning and Mom joined him the next night. I continued to care for Judy and help my father for almost two more years.

As soon as the Lord had told me to start packing and scheduling flights, I began to look for a caregiver. Two weeks before my departure I was feeling apprehensive and a little bit guilty because I still had not found anyone I could trust to take care of my family.

One morning, I asked my father if I could borrow a suitcase. He told me that there was a brand new suitcase with the tags still on it in the closet. When I reached my hand into the deep dark heater closet it felt like a fuzzy yarn tie was around the suitcase handle. When I lifted the suitcase out from the closet I was holding what I thought was a mouse. I shrieked and threw it to the floor. Instead of being a mouse, it was a dead bird.

After retrieving a paper towel from the kitchen and throwing the bird away, I began to clean up the bird poop that was splattered on the top of the suitcase. The whole situation seemed strange. I couldn't help but wonder how the sparrow had gotten into the closet, or why Dad didn't hear it flapping around and chirping. Dad quickly answered my musing when he said the sparrow must have flown in while the roofers had been repairing the roof a few weeks earlier.

When I called my friend Melissa and related the story to her, she said it made her think about how our dreams sometimes die. When I hung up I continued to think about the little song bird. It had flown into what it thought was a safe place, probably to nest. But instead of prospering—it died, silencing its song forever. I thought it was ironic that the little bird breathed its last breath on the same brand new suitcase my mother was going to fly with to Switzerland before she got meningitis and pneumonia.

In my heart I knew that if I didn't finish packing and take this opportunity to fly, my dreams (the songs God had placed inside of me) were also going to die. So now, as I sit in Virginia typing this last story, I have peace knowing that I am in God's will and that my family is being cared for.

As I look across the room I can see the suitcase sitting in the corner that the little bird laid on to take its last breathe. I am not sure where all this journey is going to take me, but I can take a deep breath and spread my wings and fly—knowing that I have adventures to experience and songs to sing, because with such an amazing God, the possibilities are limitless!

God Bless,

Jeannie

Author's Note

(Concerning my future book)

A man recently sent me a heartbreaking testimony of severe abuse he received as a child. In his letter he commented, "I chuckle when I read or listen to experts of psychology or family counselors on either TV or radio when they say victims of abuse will, themselves, become abusers. When I was being abused, I resolved internally, with passion, to be kind and gentle toward people. That's who I am today."

Part of my reply was as follows:

God is good! As we all learn sooner or later in this life, hurting and deceived people hurt people. You mentioned that it makes you chuckle when people say that people who are abused grow up to be abusers. I personally have observed three main relational scenarios in people who have not been healed from being abused: 1.) The abused person becomes an enabler or continues to be abused when they become adults. 2.) The abused person grows up to become an abuser. 3.) The abused person shuts down and isolates himself or herself. All three are consequences of lack of knowledge, unforgiveness, denial, judgment, sin, and just a whole lot of pain. I have learned that people who abuse, and adults who allow others to abuse them, believe many of the same lies I used to believe about God, their value, and relationships—lies that keep them bound and keep them repeating detrimental cycles.

To that, he replied, "I am number three."

Most of our life stories contain at least two scenarios, if not all three. At one time or another, some of us have even played all three roles. That is why it is so important to learn truth and walk in freedom.

Thankfully, both abusers and abusees can become healthy and whole and break the cycle. I am currently writing a book about the lies that kept me in abuse. In the process I have created a survey, and I am interviewing women who are either currently in abusive marriages or have come out of abusive marriages. If you would like to participate in the survey, please contact me at truthrejoices@gmail.com. Your information will be confidential, and if I do share part of your story, it will only be with your permission. Please join with me to break the cycle of abuse in the lives of men, women, and children! It's all about God's love! It's all about freedom. It's all about helping others fulfill their God given destinies!

God Bless,

Jeannie

ENDNOTES

References for Friendly Captivity
  1. Beth Moore, Daniel Lives of Integrity Words of
     Prophecy (Nashville, TN: Lifeway
     Press, 2006), p.17.
  2. Larry Huch, Free at Last (New Kensington, PA:
     Whitaker House, 2004), p 43.
  3. Flashpoint: Planets Aligned Season 1, episode 9 aired
     9/18/08

References for "S.O.S."
  1. Edward Mote, "The Solid Rock" Hymns for the Family
     of God, Nashville TN:
     Paragon Associates Inc.,1976), p 92.

References for "Stretch Marks"
  1. Kent Hovine, Creation Seminar-copyright free

References for "Disappointment"
  1. David Meece "His Love Is Reaching", Candle in the
     Rain, (Word 1987)

References for "Finding Nemo"
  1. Finding Nemo (Pixar /Walt Disney distributed by
     Bueno Vista Home entertainment
     Inc. Burbank CA, 2001)
  2. Behold What Manner of Love-© public domain, words
     and music unverified
     www.higher praise.com

References for "A Table in the Midst"
  1. Kevin Prosch "His Banner Over Me Is Love"
     (MercyPublishing, 1991)